On
Kindness

On
Kindness

ADAM PHILLIPS

and

BARBARA TAYLOR

Farrar, Straus and Giroux
New York

Farrar, Straus and Giroux
18 West 18th Street, New York 10011

Distributed in Canada by Douglas & McIntyre Ltd.
Printed in the United States of America
Originally published in slightly different form in 2009 by
Hamish Hamilton, Great Britain
Published in the United States by Farrar, Straus and Giroux
First American edition, 2009

A portion of the chapter "A Short History of Kindness"
originally appeared, in slightly different form, in *The Believer*.

Library of Congress Cataloging-in-Publication Data
Phillips, Adam.
    On kindness / Adam Phillips and Barbara Taylor.
        p. cm.
    ISBN-13: 978-0-374-22650-3 (hardcover : alk. paper)
    ISBN-10: 0-374-22650-4 (hardcover : alk. paper)
    1. Kindness.   I. Taylor, Barbara.   II. Title.

BJ1533.K5P45   2009
177'.7—dc22

                                            2008041267

Designed by Abby Kagan

www.fsgbooks.com

3   5   7   9   10   8   6   4   2

Contents

On
Kindness

Against Kindness

Kindness, or the lack of it, has been getting a lot of press recently. Media gurus lament the selfishness of our times, while newspapers regularly feature stories like the one about a wealthy stockbroker who, at the peak of his career, decided to spend his weekends doing volunteer work with deprived children. He was amazed at his own reaction. "Helping kids just makes me so happy, I feel like a different person." His astonishment is echoed in headline reports of studies of "what makes people happy," which show kindness registering much higher on the happiness scale than self-focused behavior. A recent report described an experiment carried out by the American psychologist Martin Seligman (author of *Authentic Happiness*), who recruited a group of university students to test out "philanthropy versus fun." "Guess which one gave them the bigger kick?" the reporter chortled. "I've felt that kick too, every time I buy someone a pint."

Reading these stories, we began to wonder why people today are so surprised by the blindingly obvious. Why do the pleasures of kindness astonish us? And why are stories about kindness often so corny or silly, so trivializing of the things that matter most to most people?

The pleasures of kindness were well known in the past. Kindness was mankind's "greatest delight," the Roman philosopher-emperor Marcus Aurelius declared, and thinkers and writers have echoed him down the centuries. But today, many people find these pleasures literally incredible or at least highly suspect. An image of the self has been created that is utterly lacking in natural generosity. Most people appear to believe that deep down they (and other people) are mad, bad, and dangerous to know; that as a species—apparently unlike other species of animal—we are deeply and fundamentally antagonistic to each other, that our motives are utterly self-seeking, and that our sympathies are forms of self-protection.

This book explains how and why this has come about. It shows how the kind life—the life lived in instinctive sympathetic identification with the vulnerabilities and attractions of others—is the life we are more inclined to live, and indeed is the one we are often living without letting ourselves know that this is what we are doing. People are leading secretly kind lives all the time but without a language in which to express this, or cultural support for it. Living according to our sympathies, we imagine, will weaken or overwhelm us; kindness is the saboteur of the successful life. We need to know how we have come to believe that the best lives we can lead seem to involve sacrificing the best things about ourselves; and how we have come to believe that there are pleasures greater than kindness. Kindness, we will argue in this book—not sexuality, not violence, not money—has become our forbidden pleasure. What is it about our times that makes kindness seem so dangerous?

In one sense kindness is always hazardous because it is based on a susceptibility to others, a capacity to identify with their pleasures and sufferings. Putting oneself in someone else's shoes, as the saying goes, can be very uncomfortable. But if the pleasures of kindness—like all the greatest human pleasures—are inherently perilous, they are nonetheless some of the most satisfying we possess. How have we come to repudiate them? In 1741 the Scottish philosopher David Hume, confronted by a school of philosophy that held mankind to be irredeemably selfish, lost patience. Any person foolish enough to deny the existence of human kindness had simply lost touch with emotional reality, Hume insisted: "he has forgotten the movements of his heart." How do people come to forget about kindness and the deep pleasures it gives to them?

On Kindness seeks to answer this question. Written by a historian and a psychoanalyst, it reveals the cost and, from a historical point of view, the peculiarity of modern attitudes to kindness. For nearly all of human history—up to and beyond

David Hume's day, the so-called dawn of modernity—people have perceived themselves as naturally kind. This book shows when and why this confidence evaporated and the consequences of this transformation: how in giving up on kindness—and especially our own acts of kindness—we deprive ourselves of a pleasure that is fundamental to our sense of well-being. "We mutually belong to one another," the philosopher Alan Ryan writes, and the good life is one "that reflects this truth." Today this truth has gone underground. Independence and self-reliance are now the great aspirations; "mutual belonging" is feared and unspoken; it has become one of the great taboos of our society. Why?

To answer this we begin by looking back at ideas about kindness from the classical age onward. Kindness's original meaning of kinship or sameness has stretched over time to encompass sentiments that today go by a wide variety of names—sympathy, generosity, altruism, benevolence, humanity, compassion, pity, empathy—and that in the past were known by other terms as well, notably *philanthropia* (love of mankind) and *caritas* (neighborly or brotherly love). The precise meanings of these words vary, but fundamentally they all denote what the Victorians called "open-heartedness," the sympathetic expansiveness linking self to other. "No less indiscriminate and general than the alienation between people is the desire to breach it," the German critic Theodor Adorno once wrote, suggesting that even though our alienation, our distance from other people, may make us feel safe, it also makes us sorry, as though loneliness is the inevitable cost of looking after ourselves. History shows us the manifold expressions of humanity's desire to connect, from classical celebrations of friendship, to Christian teachings on love and charity, to twentieth-century philosophies of social welfare. It also shows us the degree of human alienation, how our capacity to care for each other is inhibited by fears and rivalries with a pedigree as long as kindness itself.

For most of Western history the dominant tradition of kindness has been Christianity, which sacralizes people's generous instincts and makes them the basis of a universalist faith. For centuries, Christian *caritas* functioned as a cultural cement, binding individuals into society. But from the sixteenth century, the Christian rule "love thy neighbor as thyself" came under increasing attack from competitive individualism. Thomas Hobbes's *Leviathan* (1651)—the urtext of the new individualism—dismissed Christian kindness as a psychological absurdity. Men, Hobbes insisted, were selfish beasts who cared for nothing but their own well-being; human existence was a "warre of alle against alle." His arguments were slow to gain ground, but by the end of the eighteenth century— despite the best efforts of David Hume and others—they were becoming orthodoxy. Two centuries later it seems we are all Hobbesians, convinced that self-interest is our ruling principle. (The French psychoanalyst Lacan suggested that the Christian injunction "love thy neighbor as thyself" must be ironic, because people hate themselves.) Kindly behavior is looked upon with suspicion; public espousals of kindness are dismissed as moralistic and sentimental. "It's just human nature," we say of selfish behavior; what more can we expect? Kindness is seen either as a cover story or as a failure of nerve. Popular icons of kindness—Princess Diana, Nelson Mandela, Mother Teresa—are either worshipped as saints or gleefully unmasked as self-serving hypocrites. Prioritizing the needs of others may be praiseworthy, we think, but it is certainly not normal.

So is it time to give up on being kind? Or at least to drop kindness as one of the things we claim to value, and instead just enjoy the apparently spontaneous but fleeting moments of kindness in our lives while acknowledging that, for selfish creatures like ourselves, these moments are the exceptions that prove the rule?

Today it is only between parents and children that kindness is expected, sanctioned, and indeed obligatory. But before we condemn the mother who rages at her toddler in the street, we might stop to consider what it feels like to be a parent in a society where kindness is incidentally praised while being implicitly discouraged. Kindness—that is, the ability to bear the vulnerability of others, and therefore of oneself—has become a sign of weakness (except of course among saintly people, in whom it is a sign of their exceptionality). No one yet says parents should stop being kind to their children. Nonetheless we have become phobic of kindness in our societies, avoiding obvious acts of kindness and producing, as we do with phobias, endless rationalizations to justify our avoidance. All compassion is self-pity, D. H. Lawrence remarked, and this usefully formulates the widespread modern suspicion of kindness: that it is either a higher form of selfishness (the kind that is morally triumphant and secretly exploitative) or the lowest form of weakness (kindness is the way the weak control the strong, the kind are only kind because they haven't got the guts to be anything else). If we think of humans as essentially competitive, and therefore triumphalist by inclination, as we are encouraged to do, then kindness looks distinctly old-fashioned, indeed nostalgic, a vestige from a time when we could recognize ourselves in each other and feel sympathetic because of our kind-ness—if such a time ever existed. And what, after all, can kindness help us win, except moral approval; or possibly not even that, in a society where "respect" for personal status has become a leading value.

Most people, as they grow up now, secretly believe that kindness is a virtue of losers. But agreeing to talk about winners and losers is part and parcel of the phobic avoidance, the contemporary terror of kindness. Because one of the things the enemies of kindness never ask themselves—and this is now an enemy within all of us—is why we feel it at all. Why are we ever, in any way, moved to be kind to other people, not to mention to ourselves? Why does kindness matter to us? It is, perhaps, one of the distinctive things about kindness—unlike an abstract moral ideal, such as justice—that in the end we know exactly what it is, in most everyday situations; and yet our knowing what it is makes it easier to avoid. We usually know what the kind thing to do is—and kindness when it is done to us, and register its absence when it is not. We usually have the wherewithal to do it (kindness is not an expert skill); and it gives us pleasure. And yet we are extremely disturbed by it. We are never as kind as we want to be, but nothing outrages us more than people being unkind to us. There is nothing we feel more consistently deprived of than kindness; the unkindness of others has become our contemporary complaint. Kindness consistently preoccupies us, and yet most of us are unable to live a life guided by it.

So we are profoundly ambivalent about kindness. We love it and we fear it; we feel its absence very acutely—it is the misery of everyday life—and we resist our own kind impulses. Our predicament is not just a moral one (kindness as a neglected duty) but psychological. It is not merely that we are not as kind as we ought to be, but that it seems peculiarly difficult for us to hold on to the fact that we get powerful pleasure from our own acts of kindness. As naturally social beings, we feel with and for others, and this makes us simultaneously kind and self-regarding. But this ambivalence can be hard to sustain, both in ourselves and in our perceptions of others. Just how hard is apparent in our attitudes to children, who tend to be seen as either wholly innocent and good, and therefore corrupted by adults, or wholly bad (vicious and sexual and rivalrous) and therefore simply small members of the unpleasant human race. This polarized view of childhood has had damaging consequences.

Children, like the adults they will become, are complex creatures with, we will argue, an instinct for kindness and concern that is every bit as strong as their self-regarding instincts, about which we hear so much today. The forms kindness can take, like the forms sexuality can take, are partly learned from the societies in which we grow up, and so can be unlearned or badly taught or resisted. So it is one of the contentions of this book that children begin their lives "naturally" kind, and that something happens to this kindness as they grow up in contemporary society. This is not a new idea: over 250 years ago Jean-Jacques Rousseau made a passionate plea for the rescue of children's natural kindness from the corrupting effects of a divided society. This is a key point in the history of kindness, which is also the history of childhood. What is new perhaps is how easily people today are persuaded not to take kindness too seriously. How has something so integral and essential to ourselves become so incidental, so implausible to us?

This is a historical story—about how and why people have been talked out of their kindness—but also a psychological one, that is, a story about how vulnerability becomes traumatic to people. Everybody is vulnerable at every stage of their lives; everybody is subject to illness, accident, personal tragedy, political and economic reality. This doesn't mean that people aren't also resilient and resourceful. Bearing other people's vulnerability—which means sharing in it imaginatively and practically without needing to get rid of it, to yank people out of it—entails being able to bear one's own. Indeed it would be realistic to say that what we have in common is our vulnerability; it is the medium of contact between us, what we most fundamentally recognize in each other. Before we are sexual creatures we are vulnerable creatures; indeed the strength of our desires derives from our original helplessness and dependence.

The child's first, formative trauma is his growing acknowledgment of his need for others (in actuality the mother is as vulnerable to her need for her baby as the baby is to his need for her; parents need their children not to worry them too much). The needy child experiences a trauma of concern ("How can I take care of my mother to ensure that she takes care of me?"), which calls up his natural kindness; but this concern—and the later forms of kindness that emerge from it—is too easily turned away from. This turning away we call self-sufficiency, and when we want to pathologize it we call it narcissism. The pleasure of kindness is that it connects us with others; but the terror of kindness is that it makes us too immediately aware of our own and other people's vulnerabilities (vulnerabilities that we are prone to call failings when we are at our most frightened). Vulnerability—particularly the vulnerability we call desire—is our shared biological inheritance. Kindness, in other words, opens us up to the world (and worlds) of other people in ways that we both long for and dread. How can people, from childhood onward, feel confident enough to take such risks?

People want safety, whatever the cost. Perhaps it is one of the perils of secularization, that if we no longer believe in God—in a Being who is himself invulnerable and so is capable of protecting us—we cannot avoid confronting our own relative helplessness and need for each other. If there is no invulnerability anywhere, suddenly there is too much vulnerability everywhere. How do we deal with this? In his novel *Raw Youth* (1875), Dostoevsky describes a morning when people wake to find themselves alone in a godless universe. Instead of bewailing their loss, they turn to each other, substituting their own tenderness and concern for divine protection. Acknowledging human vulnerability, they respond to it positively. Kindness, for them, becomes a way of experiencing their vulnerability that tests the strengths and limits of their resources to deal with it. When God is dead, kindness is permitted. When God is dead, kindness is all that people have left.

So it is not that real kindness requires people to be selfless, it is rather that real kindness changes people in the doing of it, often in unpredictable ways. Real kindness is an exchange with essentially unpredictable consequences. It is a risk precisely because it mingles our needs and desires with the needs and desires of others, in a way that so-called self-interest never can. (The notion of self-interest implies that we always know what we want, by knowing what the self is and what its interests are. It forecloses discovery.) Kindness is a way of knowing people beyond our understanding of them. By involving us with strangers (even with "foreigners" thousands of miles away), as well as with intimates, it is potentially far more promiscuous than sexuality. But as we shall see, the child needs the adult—and his wider society—to help him keep faith with his kindness, that is, to help him discover and enjoy the pleasures of caring for others. The child who is failed in this regard is robbed of one of the greatest sources of human happiness. People have long known this, and long forgotten it. The history of kindness, to which we now turn, tells the story of this knowing, and forgetting, and reknowing, as central to Western ideas about the good life.

Nietzsche wrote in *The Genealogy of Morals* (1887)—the great nineteenth-century critique of the roots of morality—that he "regarded the inexorable progress of the morality of compassion which afflicted even the philosophers with its illness, as the most sinister symptom of the sinister development of our European culture." It is our view that the morality of compassion has not made progress—has indeed shied away from its shrewdest insights—and that this is the truly sinister symptom of modern life.

II

A Short History of Kindness

Kindness has always been contentious. Ancient philosophers disputed whether people were naturally kind or selfish, while Christian Fathers argued about the origins of kindness: was it intrinsic to human nature or bestowed on mankind by God? Renaissance intellectuals debated the merits of social fellowship versus the self-oriented life, while Enlightenment meditations on the theme began explosively with Thomas Hobbes's no-holds-barred defense of egoistic individualism in his *Leviathan*, which in turn met with sharp rebuttals from pro-kindness savants like David Hume, Adam Smith, and Jean-Jacques Rousseau. Modern ideas about kindness effectively begin with Hobbes and his critics, especially Rousseau, whose sophisticated psychological account of kindness presages the psychoanalytic perspectives of the Freudian era. Rousseau was the first Western thinker to recognize the importance of childhood experience in the development of the kindly self; thus, he is a key figure in this history, his insights providing a crucial bridge between past and present.

A word about pronouns: prior to the late twentieth century, when people wrote "human beings" they meant men. "He" meant everyone—masculinity was the human template, with women disappearing into the male universal. Yet ironically, one of the key outcomes of the egoism-kindness quarrel was to feminize kindness, divesting it from humanity as a whole while leaving a residue of womanly kindness, notably maternal solicitude. In recent times kindness has been largely a feminine prerogative, with men consigned to lonely egoism. Now some women, too, especially in the corporate world, are insisting on their right to be as ruthlessly competitive as men: in a dog-eat-dog world, even equality has its dark side.

In A.D. 64 the Stoic philosopher Seneca pondered friendship. The Stoics' intellectual adversaries, the Epicureans, had claimed that a man sought friends for purely instrumental reasons, "for the purpose of having someone to come and sit beside his bed when he is ill or come to his rescue when he is hard up or thrown into chains." But Seneca knew better. A wise man wanted friends "so that he may have someone by whose sickbed he himself may sit, or whom he may himself release when that person is held prisoner by hostile hands." Kindness was man's duty but also his joy: "No one can live a happy life if he turns everything to his own purposes. Live for others if you want to live for yourself."

People need other people, not just for companionship or support in hard times but to fulfill their humanity. This theme ran through all of ancient thought but was strongest among the Stoics, who propounded a moral psychology based on *oikeiôsis*, the attachment of self to other. Stoics were famously self-reliant, but the self on which a Stoic relied was not singular but communal. Stoics regarded reality as governed by a Logos, a divine principle of rationality, which manifested itself as reason in every human soul. No man was an island, as John Donne wrote centuries later; all belonged to the great "community of reason" and were precious to each other for their common humanity. The world was but a "single city," the Stoic emperor Marcus Aurelius averred, whose citizens were united by reason and "mutual affection."

Not everyone agreed with this communalism. Epicureans certainly did not, describing humanity not as a unity but as an agglomeration of individuals, each driven by self-love and the pursuit of personal pleasure. The Stoics by contrast, while acknowledging the existence of self-love, interpreted it in nonindividualist terms: each person, they argued, is born with a primary self-attachment which, as he matures into the fellowship of reason, fosters attachments to others. Aristotle had argued that friendship was self-love extended outward. The Stoics developed the idea into a concept of the self as the center point of concentric circles of *oikeiôsis*, of which the innermost circles were composed of blood relatives, followed by friends and neighbors, with the circles gradually radiating outward to encompass all humanity. Whether the degree of attachment was the same at all levels was a matter of controversy. Aristotle had described affection for humankind in general as "diffuse" and "watery" and some Stoics concurred, arguing that affective bonds increased in strength the closer the connection, with parents and children experiencing the strongest attachment while goodwill to strangers tended to be more dutiful than affectionate. The Roman statesman Cicero—not a card-carrying Stoic but much influenced by Stoicism—in his great work *De officiis* (44 B.C.) declared that it was natural to feel more kindly toward your family than anyone else. Yet elsewhere Cicero argued that warm relationships extended throughout human society, and warned that people who cared more for their fellow citizens than for foreigners threatened to "rend apart the fellowship that unites mankind."

"A man's true delight," Marcus Aurelius counseled, "is to do the things he was made for. He was made to show goodwill to his kind." In a well-ordered personality, *oikeiôsis*, whether directed at strangers or intimates, was a pleasurable virtue. Stoics were ascetics: the pleasures they endorsed were not appetitive or sensual but "soul states" that enhanced the goodness of the individual by bringing him into harmony with the oneness of nature. The naturalness of kindness, its roots in early childhood affections, made it a font of happiness that "expanded the soul." (Most Epicureans, despite Stoic claims to the contrary, also believed something like this, with Epicurus writing in extravagant terms about the joys of friendship, "which dances around the world.")

This joyous element in pro-kindness thought was suppressed by post-Augustinian Christianity. Kindness became linked, disastrously, to self-sacrifice, which made it a sitting duck for philosophical egoists such as Thomas Hobbes, who could easily demonstrate that self-sacrifice was rarely practiced, even by its most ardent proponents. Pagan kindness, by contrast, had no truck with self-sacrifice. The pleasures of kindness, as Enlightenment pagans like David Hume and Adam Smith were later to insist, were powerful because they derived from the natural sociality of man. People were kind not because they were told to be but because it made them feel fully human. To "love one another" was a joyous expression of one's humanity, not a Christian duty.

Yet the transition from pagan society to Christianity was a key moment in the history of kindness. Pagan kindness developed against a background of long-standing distinctions between freemen and slaves, high and low, rich and poor, men and women, citizens and foreigners. Few thinkers, even among the Stoics, challenged these divisions; instead, they incorporated them into a concept of humanity that was not general but exemplary. Only the man who displayed reason and fitness for civilized society—which in turn required wealth and standing—was regarded as fully human. Tensions between this gentlemanly definition of humanness and a more inclusive version were present in ancient thought, although barely acknowledged by its spokesmen. Yet it was these tensions that would make the advent of Christianity so explosive. With Christianity, humanness suddenly belonged to everyone, even women (although the terms on which women possessed it were markedly different from those of men). And kindness, too, became generalized, the prescribed mode of relating across the entire human family.

The development of Christianity from a Jewish sect into a universalist faith was marked by a strong assertion of kindly values. Adopting the Greek word for love, *agape*, Christian teachers described it as a divine love that, flowing from heaven into the human soul, irradiated the soul with *caritas*. To "love thy neighbor as thyself" was the great moral law. "But who is my neighbor?" a man is reported to have asked Jesus. Jesus replied by telling him about a traveling Israelite who, beset by robbers and left injured by the roadside, is ignored by all passersby, including some fellow Israelites, until finally a Samaritan takes pity on him and assists him with consummate generosity. Israelites and Samaritans were long-standing enemies, and the parable of the Good Samaritan became, as it remains, the emblematic account of Christian kindness, of sympathies that overleap ethnic barriers and sectarian divisions to turn all people into friends and neighbors. By universalizing kindness, Christianity staked its claim to be a global faith: a theme that reached a pinnacle in the writings of St. Augustine, who in his *City of God* (A.D. 426) argued for a "Holy charity" to encompass "the whole world," pagans and sinners as well as God's faithful: "A man's friends are

[all] with whom [he] is joined by membership of the human society."

Coupled with Jesus' attacks on wealth and privilege, this version of kindness was potentially—and sometimes actually—highly inimical to established orders. Throughout its history, institutional Christianity has had to wrestle with the subversive implications of *caritas*. The growth of ecclesiastical power, from the second century, generated powerful tensions. The paradox of an increasingly hierarchical Church preaching universal brotherhood was not lost on low-ranking members of the faith. A host of movements arose—from the Cathars of medieval France to the Anabaptist rebels of sixteenth-century Münster and the Diggers of Cromwellian England—determined to build a New Jerusalem of loving fraternity here on earth. The suppression of such movements and the sponsorship of savage campaigns against heretics and infidels often made *caritas* seem a distant dream. In 1649 the Digger leader Gerrard Winstanley, after being attacked and driven from his home, lamented the "selfish imaginations" of power-hungry men who sought "to teach and rule over" their fellows.

These were difficult contradictions, but there was an even deeper dilemma at the heart of Christian kindness. "If we love one another, God dwelleth in us, and his love is perfected in us," St. John sermonized. But if love derived exclusively from God, what did that imply about man? As the prophet of love, Christ promised a world ruled by *caritas*. But interpreters of Christ's message in the centuries after his death reiterated all the old arguments about human nature: Were people naturally generous, or egoistical? Was *caritas* a human virtue, or a divine bestowal? The Good Samaritan parable strongly implied that kindness was a natural human disposition, and some early Christian thinkers endorsed this. But the claim was vehemently denied by St. Augustine and other Church Fathers who insisted that *caritas* emanated from God alone; that without God man had no kindness nor any other innate virtue. With the Fall, Augustine argued, mankind had lost all possibility of natural goodness. Augustinian man, sunk in original sin, was incapable of experiencing *caritas* without divine assistance; left to themselves, Adam's children were selfish reprobates.

With Augustine, *caritas* became identified with the transcendence of self. Without self-suppression and self-sacrifice, man's relationship to man, it was declared, was irrevocably vicious and bestial: a bleak vision of humankind that with the sixteenth-century Protestant Reformation became very much darker. Human nature as conceived by the Reformation leader Martin Luther was "wholly spoiled and perverted" by original sin. The corruption of the Catholic priesthood demonstrated how easily individuals were seduced away from true religion by pomp and power until they sank into total depravity. Luther's disciple John Calvin was even more ferociously antihuman. Man, according to Calvin, was a "satanic creature," a "vile polluted lump of earth" whose every impulse was selfish and rotten. Who could love such a worm? The philosopher Jean-Jacques Rousseau spent his childhood in Calvinist Geneva. The Christian preacher, he later wrote, shows

> all men as monsters to be stifled, as victims of the Devil whose company can only corrupt the heart and cast us into Hell. And what is most peculiar after all of these beautiful declamations, the same man gravely exhorts us to love our neighbors, that is, this whole troop of rascals from whom he has inspired us with such horror.

All men, whatever their virtuous pretensions, deserved to burn. Only individuals elected by God for salvation would escape this judgment, and even these lucky elect were encouraged to look on each other with suspicion, wary of false claims and moral backsliding. The true saint was counseled to trust no one, not even his spouse or close friends. This attitude has left some vicious legacies: the hatred of present-day right-wing Protestants for "liberals" and "secularists" has a very long pedigree with little kindness in it.

The Protestant Reformation demoted kindness from its foremost place in Christian moral self-understanding. Protestant *caritas*, with some notable exceptions, was institutionalized and limited—charity in its modern sense. Early-modern Protestants made excellent businessmen, as the sociologist Max Weber showed, but the commercial spirit was not a generous one. And the brutal religious conflicts of the seventeenth century did little to enhance the Christian reputation for brotherly love. A secularizing wave began to move through

European intellectual circles, and human nature was loosened from its religious moorings. Hobbes's *Leviathan* reflected the change of mood. *Leviathan* was published in the immediate wake of the English Puritan revolution and reverberated with the horrors of civil conflict, portraying the world as a battleground of ruthless egoists competing for "riches, honour, command" in an unremitting "warre of alle against alle." An avowed materialist, Hobbes depicted human beings not as wayward souls but as pleasure-maximizing machines driven solely by self-concern and "a perpetual and restless desire of power after power that ceaseth only in death." To scandalized critics who condemned such a vision as amoral and unchristian, Hobbes's response was uncompromising: "It may seem strange that Nature should thus render man apt to invade, and destroy one another . . . [but I] do not accuse man's nature in it. The Desires and other Passions of man are in themselves no sin." We must take man as he is, was the chilling message: there is no point in protesting against human nature.

With Hobbes, selfishness and aggression were transformed from moral vices into psychological facts. The pursuit of pleasure, so long condemned by Christian moralists, was naturalized into a primary instinct, the engine of all human action. Similar ideas were propounded by enlightened Epicureans in France, and their combined influence was enormous. While Enlightenment thinkers across Europe expressed revulsion at Hobbes's misanthropy and moral pessimism, most accepted his hedonistic premises. Prophets of the commercial system, such as the Scottish philosopher Adam Smith, approved individual pleasure-seeking while denying that it generated social conflict. The great advantage of capitalism, according to Smith, was that it turned individual desires to public benefit. The businessman looking for high profits, the worker seeking a living wage, the buyer avid for new consumer products: under capitalism, thanks to the operations of the free market (Smith's famous "hidden hand"), all these individuals, whatever their motives, contributed to each other's well-being and thus to universal prosperity. "It is not from the benevolence of the butcher, the brewer, or the baker that we expect our dinner, but from their regard to their own interest," Smith wrote in *Wealth of Nations* (1776), yet it was the combined self-love of these traders that guaranteed the nation its dinners. "Sweet commerce," as its admirers dubbed it, was inherently benevolent.

But if self-love was validated by the Enlightenment, selfishness emphatically was not. Pleasure-seeking was never to be at the expense of others. In the face of the Hobbesian challenge, defenders of kindness rose to insist that true pleasure was always generous. Enlightened Anglicans led the way, repudiating original sin and describing *caritas* as a natural disposition to gain pleasure from the happiness of others. Christian morality had long been at odds with natural human impulses, but now a new wave of clerics celebrated mankind's spontaneous generosity. "As all the actions of nature are sweet and pleasant," one wrote sometime before 1720, "so there is none which gives a good man a greater pleasure than acts of kindness or charity." The theme was taken up by moral philosophers who translated this natural *caritas* into a kindly instinct or sense on par with the other natural senses. "If any Appetite or Sense be natural, the Sense of Fellowship is the same," the leading Enlightener Lord Shaftesbury declared. Benevolence—the Enlightenment buzzword for kindness and all its cognates—was a primitive instinct, the Scottish philosopher Francis Hutcheson wrote, against whose delights the pleasures of self-love paled by comparison. "To be kind is the greatest measure of human happiness."

The idea became hugely popular in the eighteenth century, prompted by unease about the socially divisive effects of capitalist development. In an increasingly profit-driven, competitive world, new sources of social adhesion were needed, and natural kindness—enthusiastically promoted in sermons, poetry, conduct books, and novels—was well suited to the task. Psychological egoists remained plentiful, but alongside them appeared a veritable army of "benevolists," their hearts throbbing with "social affection" and "practical philanthropy." The results were dramatic. A wave of humanitarian activism swept Britain and America, tackling evils—such as slavery, child neglect, and cruelty to animals—that long had been ignored or defended. "Friends of mankind" marched across the social landscape, leaving in their wake a rich institutional and ideological legacy. This was benevolence at its best. At its worst—and the worst became very evident as the century progressed—it descended into a mawkish cult of tenderheartedness much ridiculed by satirists. "I love to see a gentleman with a tender heart," the predatory bailiff Timothy Twitch declared in Oliver Goldsmith's *The Good Natured Man* (1768). "Moral weeping" became the vogue, especially among women who preened themselves on their extreme softheartedness. Skeptics had a field day mocking sentimentalists who wept over orphaned puppies while paying their servants starvation wages. William Blake captured the hypocrisy perfectly in "The Human Abstract":

> *Pity would be no more*
> *If we did not make somebody poor,*
> *And Mercy no more could be*
> *If all were as happy as we.*

Were those Hobbesian skeptics right, then, who regarded all acts of kindness as selfishness in disguise?

Enlightenment ideas about kindness exposed a dilemma at the heart of Western attitudes to human nature. For most of its premodern history, stretching into the Enlightenment, kindness had been treated as the solution to a problem: the problem of other people. Self and other were seen as separate entities with kindness serving as a bridge between them, modifying the claims of self in favor of the other, and thereby promoting goodwill and social solidarity. But kindness as an individual attribute could never escape the prison of ego. As the property of an insular self, kindness was always going to be a very limited emotion, prone to collapsing into what Thomas Carlyle later derided as the "tumultuous frothy ocean-tide of benevolent sentimentality." But there was an alternative Enlightenment account of kindness that avoided these dangers, by treating self and other as interdependent. Here the self was seen not as isolated but as inherently social, formed through its kindly relations with others. It is this version of kindness—enriched and complicated by psychoanalytic insights on human motivation—that is at the heart of this book. Its origins lie in the concept of sympathy, as developed by a group of Scottish philosophers (notably David Hume and Adam Smith) but above all by the man who is probably the greatest kindness theorist of Western thought, the wild man of the Enlightenment, Jean-Jacques Rousseau.

"Sympathy" today means pity or compassion, but for all of the eighteenth and most of the nineteenth century it was a much larger concept, referring to a mutual sharing of feelings among people—literally, "fellow feeling." Where both egoists such as Hobbes and benevolists such as Lord Shaftesbury perceived individuals as self-enclosed worlds, sympathy theorists regarded them as affectively linked, with the emotional life of an individual evolving under the direct influence of the feelings of those around him. Subjectivity was interpersonal, and it was this that made kindness possible. In his *Treatise of Human Nature* (1739–40), David Hume compared the transmission of feelings between people to the vibration of violin strings, with each individual resonating with the pains and pleasures of others as if they were his own. We are "taken out of ourselves" into the emotional worlds of others,

Hume wrote; or, as Adam Smith put it in his *Theory of Moral Sentiments* (1759), "We become in some measure the same person . . . this is the source of our fellow feeling." Psychological egoists had claimed that fellow feeling was merely an offshoot of self-concern, arising from fear that whatever befell someone else might befall us, too. Smith denied this, arguing that fellow feeling was an imaginative projection of self into other: we "enter as it were into his body." To egoists who replied that this was just a more complex form of selfishness, Smith's response was robust: How could any emotion be regarded as selfish that is "not in the least upon my account" but "which is entirely occupied by what relates to you"? People who espoused the egoist position were simply confused about human nature, Smith insisted.

The sympathetic self was an expansive self, one for whom the happiness of others was the sine qua non of its own well-being. Sympathy was a touchstone of humanity; a person incapable of sympathetic identification with his or her fellows was inhuman, a monstrosity. Many Enlightenment thinkers propounded ideas like these, but it was Jean-Jacques Rousseau who turned them into a psychology of kindness of unparalleled sophistication and influence.

Rousseau seems an unlikely prophet of kindness. Cantankerous and solitary, Rousseau was notoriously self-absorbed. "He is everything to himself," he wrote of himself. "There never was a man on earth less curious about what doesn't touch him." But what in others might be mindless egoism, in Rousseau bred a forensic fascination with his inner life that yielded extraordinary insights. He was easily touched, and everything that touched him aroused profound curiosity. Every experience, every encounter—no matter how slight or evanescent—was probed for its meanings and hidden significance. No relationship, including his relationship with himself, was free from inquisitional scrutiny.

Pain was the spur. Other people were always a painful conundrum for Rousseau. In his *Confessions* (1782–89) he portrayed himself as one whose intensely affectionate disposition made him uniquely susceptible to indifference or cruelty. Narcissism was a flight from pain. "We are never," Freud wrote many years later, "so defenseless against suffering as when we love." But it was Rousseau who first anatomized this vulnerability that he felt so acutely. "All my misfortunes come from my need to attach my heart.... It is only when I am alone that I am my own master." Toward the end of his life, after decades of disappointment and misery, isolation seemed the only viable option, although, as human happiness is ineluctably social, this was no happy choice: "One is never able to enjoy oneself without the cooperation of another."

That people need other people is hardly news, but for Rousseau this dependence extended far beyond companionship or even love, into the very process of becoming human. Rousseau believed that people are not born but made, every individual a bundle of potentials whose realization entails the active involvement of other people. Self-development is a social process. Self-sufficiency is an impossible fantasy. Much of the time Rousseau wished passionately that it were not: *Robinson Crusoe* was a favorite book, and he yearned to be free from the pains and uncertainties of social life. But his writings document with extraordinary clarity the shaping of the individual by his emotional attachments. "Our sweetest existence is relative and collective, and our true *self* is not entirely within us." And it is kindness—which Rousseau analyzed under the rubric of *pitié*, which translates as "pity" but is much closer to "sympathy" as Hume and Smith defined it—that is the key to this collective existence.

Society corrupts: this is Rousseau's famous message. Man enters the world as an openhearted innocent and society perverts him into a monster of selfishness. It is this tragic narrative that frames Rousseau's account of kindness. Man is born with the instinctual self-love necessary for his survival (*amour de soi*), but entry into society, with its vicious inequalities and rivalries, transforms this innate self-concern into *amour propre*, a "hateful and irascible" egoism based on the envious comparison of self to others. A man raised in a simple, natural manner will be full of affection for himself and all those around him, especially for those who are kind to him. But social man, the man of the world, is full of "cruel and repulsive passions" that "contract the heart and tighten the spring of the human I." All men are born naked and vulnerable; all are condemned to die. The natural man, feeling his oneness with his fellows, looks upon them with sympathy. His "expansive heart" extends itself toward them; he cries with their pain, sighs with their suffering. But the worldly man yearns for preeminence and his *pitié* withers under this ambition.

Is this fall inevitable? Often Rousseau seemed to imply that it was. In his early writings he portrayed *pitié* as a primitive instinct that disappeared as the individual became civilized. Only mothers, young children, and uncivilized peoples ("savages") remained capable of feeling it. But a later work, *Emile* (1762), told a more (complicatedly) optimistic story.

Emile, the eighteenth century's most famous work on childhood, imagines the maturation of a boy educated to follow his natural inclinations instead of social conventions. Emile is raised to be kind. The idea that children might be naturally kind was very unusual in the eighteenth century. Christian dogmatists portrayed children as steeped in selfishness, from which only God's grace could redeem them, and Enlightenment writers such as John Locke naturalized this account. "We see Children," Locke wrote, "as soon almost as they are born, cry, grow peevish, sullen, out of humour, for nothing but to have their *Wills*. They would have their Desires submitted to by others . . . pleasing themselves with the Power that seems to give." In *Emile*, Rousseau sharply criticized this description, arguing that the egoism Locke attributed to children was not natural but socially induced. Children are "naturally inclined to benevolence," but society thwarts this innate disposition, replacing it with competitive egoism. But every child must enter society: how is natural kindness to be preserved?

With difficulty, was Rousseau's answer; and the brilliance of his account lies in his anatomization of this difficulty. In *Emile*, the vicissitudes of kindness are one and the same as the perils of personhood. The self is formed through relations with others, Rousseau shows, and *pitié* is the emotional agent of this process.

Pitié in *Emile* is shown to develop through two phases, a prepubescent instinctual phase and a relational phase that begins with puberty. As a small child, Emile feels an instinctive *pitié* for his parents and other caretakers that is "purely mechanical," an automatic reflex of his self-preservative drives (*amour de soi*). Surrounded by people, Emile is nonetheless psychically alone, experiencing his family not as thinking and feeling beings like himself but as mere instruments of his needs. His *pitié* is just an extension of his self-love. His imagination is dormant, and other people appear only as more or less useful things to him. "He loves his sister as he loves his watch."

Thus oblivious to the humanity of those around him, Emile is likewise unconscious of his own: "He does not feel himself to be of any sex, of any species." The prepubescent child has "nature's ignorance" of gender; he knows nothing of the passions that will later make sexual differences so intensely interesting to him. "Man and woman are equally alien to him." His fantasy life is quiescent, and he is indifferent to adult interactions. But with the approach of puberty all this changes. Now erotic sensations awake Emile's imagination, and with this comes an onrush of "social feeling." *Pitié* enters its relational phase.

> The child, not imagining what others feel, knows no ills but his own, but when the first development of the senses lights the fire of imagination, he begins to feel himself in others, to be moved by their pleas, and to suffer their ills. It is then that the sad tableau of suffering humanity must bring to his heart the first compassion it has ever experienced.

With the arousal of the adolescent imagination, Emile's inner world opens to admit other people. Awareness of species-belonging is born, and with it *pitié* in its fully human form. All animals feel an instinctive pity ("It is so natural that the very brutes give evidence of it") but only in mankind does pity require fantasy to activate it, because only in man does it take the form of an imaginary transportation of self into other. "How do we let ourselves be moved by pity if not by transporting ourselves outside of ourselves and identifying with the sufferer; by leaving, as it were, our own being to take on its being?" The pitying imagination replaces the narcissistic cocoon of infancy with an other-oriented self, born through desire and fantasy. The "expansive heart" finds itself "everywhere outside of itself," in other people whose vulnerable humanity awakens its own. Subjectivity becomes populated as infantile self-love evolves into a social "sensitivity" that is no mere instinct, much less a lifestyle option, but a condition of development into full personhood.

Pitié is the midwife of true selfhood. The Hobbesian man, the man who "feels only himself," is not a true man but a brute. Yet Rousseau was no sentimentalist. Kindness, Emile soon discovers, is not the only way people respond to each other. Human beings are profoundly ambivalent creatures, whose sensitivity to others can make them "hateful and cruel" as well as "loving and gentle." "It is not in the human heart to put ourselves in the place of people who are happier than we." People happier than ourselves are likelier to arouse envy than sympathy, Rousseau points out; we must perceive individuals as subject to the same ills as ourselves if we are to identify with them. Desiring people, especially for sex, is very often inimical to kindness, especially when the desired person resists our overtures. The helpless dependence of the would-be lover on his beloved can breed rage and hatred. (Freudians later had plenty to say about this intimate connection between erotic desire and aggression.) Most important, identifying with other people risks obliterating them as separate beings. We must feel the sufferings of others as theirs, not ours, if we are to retain a sense of their alterity. Emile, Rousseau writes,

> shares the suffering of his fellow-creatures, but he shares it of his own free will and finds pleasure in it. He enjoys at once the pity he feels for their woes and the joy of being exempt from them; he feels in himself that state of vigor which projects us beyond ourselves, and bids us carry elsewhere the superfluous activity of our well-being. To pity

another's woes we must indeed know them, but we need not feel them.

Emile becomes a person by imaginatively identifying with others, but he and they remain separate beings. His vitality serves to maintain the self/other boundary, even as fantasy leaps this divide. He enjoys feeling pity for others because it reminds him of his own aliveness (which makes sympathy easy for him). Implicit in this complex and compelling story is Rousseau's assumption that an individual's capacity for kindness depends on the strength of his *amour de soi*, his healthy self-love. Only the child who revels in his own well-being will "seek to extend his being and enjoyments" to others. Only a vigorous, self-caring child can afford to pity others without feeling overwhelmed by their woes and so end up hating them. Emile, educated according to nature, is such a child— but he is a fiction, a product of Rousseau's imagination. Could such a boy really exist? Emile's egoism is depicted as warm and generous, but in the real world—as Rousseau saw it—men's egoism ran very cold. Torn from nature, plunged into savage rivalry, modern men had lost not just their kindness, but themselves: "They don't know how to love themselves; they only know how to hate what is not themselves."

Hardly an upbeat vision, then, but one of deep psychological acuity and lasting significance, whose influence in the final years of the eighteenth century became literally revolutionary.

Rousseau was a radical who identified strongly with the marginal and powerless. But he was no Emile. Grandiose yet profoundly insecure, he committed acts of exceptional callousness during his life (including placing all five of his babies in orphanages because, he claimed, his wife's family would have ruined them). Nonetheless, for generations of readers he was the age's great oracle of kindness. Political radicals in particular celebrated him as a "divine" philosopher whose dedication to the "good of his fellow beings" (in Maximilien Robespierre's words) inspired lovers of mankind everywhere. Rousseau died a decade before the French Revolution, but with its outbreak his reputation rocketed, as revolutionaries looked to his writings for blueprints of the good society. Encomiums to his virtue and generosity proliferated until he achieved cultlike status. Meanwhile, conservatives denounced him as a mealy-mouthed hypocrite who preached universal love while abusing his friends and family. By the mid-1790s he had become the leading icon of revolutionary kindness, loved and loathed in equal measure for his "tender" philosophy.

This elevation of a cranky, self-absorbed genius into an emblem of radical benevolence was symptomatic of the times. Kindness had always possessed a subversive edge, and at the end of the eighteenth century this potential exploded. Kindness became a political battleground as radicals across Europe and Britain promoted "universal benevolence" as the emotional foundation stone of republican democracy while conservatives attacked them for philanthropic extremism. Churches rang with controversy as left-wing clerics called on all kind hearts to embrace the principles of the Revolution, prompting their right-wing opponents to condemn social love as "more subversive against society than open warfare." "Brotherly love must embrace only brethren," an English bishop declared. People were urged to put traditional loyalties—to family, class, nation—ahead of affection for humankind in general. Leave universal happiness to God, they were instructed, instead of the "mad democratical schemes" of revolutionary benevolists.

But for a time it seemed as if the benevolists might have their way. In the heady early years of the Revolution, it appeared to many that a kinder world was about to be born. The descent into terror destroyed such dreams. Conservatives crowed at the spectacle of erstwhile apostles of brotherly love marching each other to the scaffold, an image so dismaying that many progressive-minded people outside France also turned away in disgust. Universal kindness lost its reformist luster, and a new wave of philosophical egoism swept intellectual circles. Political economists who had earlier sought to portray commercial activity as altruistic openly defended unbridled self-interest. Christian *caritas* was siphoned off into philanthropic activity aimed at assisting the "deserving poor" while ensuring that the plebs remained submissive and deferential. To be treated kindly by one's superiors was a privilege, not a right, humble folk were reminded.

In 1798, as the Revolution moved toward its close, the political economist Thomas Malthus published his *Essay on the Principle of Population*, one of the most influential texts of

Western modernity. Malthus was determined to show that any society governed by benevolist principles was doomed to poverty and misery. Human beings procreate as fast as their income permits, he argued. Therefore, any attempt to improve the general condition of society was demographically doomed. Abolishing poverty and inequality would lead to overpopulation and universal want. State-sponsored charity like the Poor Laws, which gave support to the unemployed, just encouraged the poor to overbreed. Benevolence may be "one of the noblest qualities of the human heart," he conceded, but egoism was the engine of human progress. "It is to the apparently narrow principle of self-love that we are indebted for all the noblest exertions of human genius . . . for everything, indeed, that distinguishes the civilized from the savage state; and no sufficient change has as yet taken place in the nature of civilised man to enable us to say that he . . . may safely throw down the ladder by which he has risen to this eminence." Fed by free-market ideology, the argument rapidly swelled in influence. Advanced opinion embraced "enlightened self-interest" (and the abolition of the Poor Laws), and champions of kindness were thrown sharply on the defensive.

Thus, by the opening of the nineteenth century, the long quarrel between kindness and egoism had begun to turn decisively in egoism's favor. A bullish capitalism harnessed to counterrevolution pushed kindness from the moral center. Kindness was steadily downgraded from a universal imperative to the prerogative of specific social constituencies: romantic poets, clergymen, charity workers, and—above all—

women, whose presumed tenderheartedness survived the egoist onslaught. By the end of the Victorian period, kindness had been largely feminized, ghettoized into a womanly sphere of feeling and behavior where it has remained, with some notable exceptions, ever since.

This privileged association of women with kindness was not new. Like all emotions, kindness had always raised tricky questions about which feelings were suitable for which sex. From antiquity on, pro-kindness thinkers had worried that too much sympathy might undermine manly gravitas. Moderate affection and compassion were excellent, but to be overwhelmed by concern for others was regarded as a feminine failing. As the irrational sex, women were naturally prone to sympathetic incontinence, while men, as the ruling sex, had to retain self-command. "For one's mind to yield to pity is an effect of affability, gentleness, and softness," the French essayist Michel de Montaigne wrote in 1580. "That is why weaker natures such as women are more subject to them."

To "yield" to kindness was feebly feminine. This derogatory association of women with kindness persisted into the modern age. But alongside it ran the Judeo-Christian celebration of maternal love as the epitome of natural kindness: a theme so powerful in Western thought that even staunch egoists acceded to it. "For who," as one late seventeenth-century Hobbesian wrote, "can doubt the affection of a mother for her helpless infant? No heart beats more tenderly than hers." During the Enlightenment, these ideas received a quasi-scientific gloss, as investigations into the female character purported to show women as more instinctively attuned to the needs and feelings of others than men. Idealizations of maternal kindness spread to encompass women in general, whose intuitive humanity became a leitmotif of enlightened thought. New gender distinctions were introduced, with higher forms of benevolence—magnanimity, public spiritedness—assigned to men while women were consigned to spontaneous, unreflective modes of kindness. The distinction was untenable, but philosophers struggled hard to maintain it, including Rousseau, who drew a contrast between Emile's self-enlarging, imaginative *pitié* and primitive, instinctive *pitié*, which he assigned to mothers, babies, and savages. In Rousseau's day, "savages," that is, "nonwhite races," were routinely described as kindly creatures, but by the early nineteenth century, with Western nations struggling to justify black colonial slavery, savages were generally regarded as cold-blooded and aggressive. Women's superior sympathy and compassion, however, suffered no such diminution, becoming rather an idée fixe of the age. A cult of feminine kindness arose, underpinned by the Victorian ideal known as the "angel in the house." Consigned to a private, domestic existence, women became a repository of all those other-regarding emotions inappropriate to the competitive hurly-burly of male society. Safely sequestered in the female heart, far from boardrooms and battlefields, kindness became as crucial to women as an unblemished sexual reputation, and as socially irrelevant.

All good women (and occasional bad ones, like the softhearted whores of popular fiction) participated in this idealization, but mothers were the exemplars. The mother/child bond was the quintessence of kindness. And what of the child in this model dyad? Here the influence of Rousseau was strongly felt. By the end of the eighteenth century, thanks largely to Rousseau, the sinful child of Christian tradition was being overtaken by his alter ego, the innocent cherub who, in a much simplified version of Rousseau's message, was portrayed as instinctively generous and untainted by the egoistical rivalries of adulthood. A host of nineteenth-century poets and novelists celebrated the openheartedness of infancy, that "seed-time of the soul," in William Wordsworth's phrase, when native affections flowed unimpeded by worldly considerations. The withering of this generosity, under the malign influence of selfish adults, became an emblem of modern corruption. In many Victorian novels the "warm young hearts" of children (in Charles Dickens's phrase) appeared as the last refuge of kindness in a cruel society, a reproachful reminder to adult readers of a "heaven they have lost."

Autobiographies of Victorian luminaries took up this theme, exploring the importance of kindness in the childhood experience. The great liberal philosopher John Stuart Mill learned about unkindness at a young age. His early years were blighted by his father, the Utilitarian philosopher James Mill, who preached brotherly love while treating his own son with stern coldness. John Stuart grew into a youth with a theoretical devotion to mankind but no "genuine benevolence." At twenty he collapsed into a deep depression, from which he eventually rescued himself by reading Wordsworth's poetry, which gave him a "greatly increased interest in the common feelings and common destiny of human beings." His later love affair with and marriage to Harriet Taylor, whom he regarded as a paragon of generosity, sealed the transformation, and he became an advocate of "altruism," a term first coined in the 1850s by the French philosopher Auguste Comte, who developed a complex theory of benevolence as a neurological function. (Other influential recruits to Comtean altruism included the writers George Eliot and Harriet Martineau, and the philosopher Henry Sidgwick.) The embrace of altruism reshaped Mill's politics, and he abandoned liberalism for socialism. "The deep rooted selfishness which forms the general character of the existing state of society," he wrote of the capitalist system, "is *so* deeply rooted, only because the whole course of existing institutions tends to foster it."

Mill was one of many Victorians to mount a valiant defense of kindness against the increasing individualism of the age. Throughout the second half of the nineteenth century, a variety of religious and secular moralists—altruists, humanitarians, Christian socialists—urged the claims of the social principle against those of the selfish principle. Faced with a widespread loss of faith among mid- and late-Victorian intellectuals, Comteans advocated a Religion of Humanity that would promote brotherly love without superstitious baggage. Malthusian political economy, the Thatcherism of its day, was a particular bête noire of these benevolists, condemned for its mechanical approach to human affairs and its ruthless attitude to the poor and vulnerable. Charles Dickens, in his novel

Hard Times (1854), portrayed political economy as disguised sadism, while Thomas Carlyle thundered against its marketization of all human relations: "To what shifts is poor Society reduced in epochs when Cash Payment has become the sole nexus of man to man!" The "coldness" of the economic mind-set, implicitly associated with men, was continually contrasted with the warm kindliness of women, whose instinctive willingness to sacrifice personal interest to the needs of others was adduced by feminists as a key rationale for female enfranchisement. Women's "intelligent sympathy," feminists claimed, would counteract male selfishness to create a kinder, gentler Britain.

These were influential voices, but the tide was running against them. Moreover, the kindness they espoused was in important respects very limited. Like many benevolists before them, these men and women valued kindness as an emotional bridge between otherwise insular individuals. Rousseau's great insight—that the human self is no isolate but a social entity, formed through relations with others; that kindness is part of the fabric of human subjectivity—was forgotten. So, too, was the eighteenth-century emphasis on the pleasurableness of kindness, which disappeared in favor of the traditional Christian opposition between self-gratification and care for others. Kindness at the end of the nineteenth century meant self-denial, an ethos highly vulnerable to the dominant egoism of the age—especially as pleasure itself became increasingly egoistical. Enlightenment pleasure had been a multifaceted emotion operating along a hierarchy that had other-regarding feelings at its apex and self-focused gratifications right down at the bottom. But in the course of the nineteenth century pleasure steadily contracted to its erotic dimension, moving away from the tender heart to the enflamed genitals. Many factors combined to produce this sexualization of pleasure, but its most consequential articulation was in the new science of psychoanalysis. With Freud and his followers, pleasure, including the pleasures of kindness, became all about sex.

III

How Kind?

When we move to a psychoanalytic account of kindness—psychoanalysis being one among many "psychologies" that emerged in the late nineteenth century—we find, unsurprisingly, many links with earlier ideas about how people want to treat each other, and what they should do about it. What sort of kindness, if any, are we capable of? What do we owe to one another, and what do we want to give to one another? Psychoanalytic reflections on these questions extend the conversation begun by Rousseau and continued in the nineteenth century—by Wordsworth and Dickens, to take two of the most prominent figures—about sociability as an expression of the bonds between parents and children, especially mothers and children. Kindness is portrayed by these writers as originating in the individual's earliest relationships; it is seen as an innate potential that society tends to thwart and corrupt. One of the more utopian implications of this view is that if there were less of a discrepancy between the way mothers treat their young children and the way relationships are conducted between adults, this world might be a more benign place. Either the natural kindness between mothers and children is a bad and misleading way of preparing the child for reality, or we should be working to make the reality of the social world more like a good family. Why are mothers and children often kinder to each other than to anyone else? How does this happen, and can anything be done to the social order to avert it?

Psychoanalysis continues the older discussion about mothers and children but then has something modern to say about human nature that accounts for, or at least attempts to describe, the fate of kindness in the developing child. Psychoanalysis adds a link between the fate of kindness and sexuality, and through the consideration of sexuality provides a revised account of human aggression. What Freud proposed, and the British pediatrician and psychoanalyst Donald Winnicott later elaborated in his own unusual way, was the idea that aggression itself can be a form of kindness; that when aggression isn't envious rage or the revenge born of humiliation, it contains the wish for a more intimate exchange, a profounder, more unsettling kindness between people. In short, psychoanalysis makes sentimentality and nostalgia, not hatred, the enemies of kindness.

It is now generally assumed that people are basically selfish and that fellow feeling is either a weakness or a luxury or a more sophisticated form of selfishness. In this picture, kindness becomes something we are nostalgic about, a longing for something that we fear may not really exist. And yet, of course, we cannot imagine childhood or parenting without it. Indeed, it is in parenting that kindness has its moment and is seen as something that adults are more capable of than children, as if kindness itself, and all that it entails, is a developmental achievement. In short, only an adult, who has learned to bear frustration, is capable of putting the needs of someone else before her own. The once-celebrated kindness of the child today tends to be ignored, sentimentalized, or pathologized. Fellow feeling does not come, as we say, naturally.

There is a strange confusion here: On the one hand, we experience our feeling for others—our identification with other people's sufferings and pleasures—as among our most immediate experiences, as though to feel for others is akin to an instinct or a reflex, as if we automatically know people to be essentially the same as ourselves. On the other hand, many of our most compelling accounts of ourselves are about our aversion or resistance or terror of this very experience. At its strongest we have come to believe that feeling too much for others—being too sympathetic—either endangers our lives or is against our nature. And in its more insidious versions we have come to suspect that the whole notion of kindness is a cover story—indeed, our most subtly self-deceiving cover story—for an ingeniously ruthless self-interest. Fellow feeling is good as long as we don't have too much of it and recognize that it isn't really fellow feeling at all. Religious people may still attach great significance to it, but among the secular-

minded the case for kindness tends to be made only skepti-
cally, with a knowing wink about the realities of human
egoism.

Psychoanalysis inherits and tries to make sense of these
muddled notions. In the process, psychoanalysis has become,
among many other things, a new story about what brings
people together and what breaks them apart. A story, in other
words, about the possibilities of fellow feeling made more
complicated by the Freudian conjecture that the very thing
that draws people to each other (sexual desire) also generates
insupportable rivalries and antagonisms, of which love and
kindness then become casualties. We must love, as Freud famously said, in order not to fall ill, and it is loving that makes
us ill. In what sense, we might wonder, does kindness make us
ill? From a psychoanalytic point of view, what are the dangers of fellow feeling?

There is a difference, psychoanalysis will tell us, between
kindness as a moral obligation and as a desire. Perceived as a
duty, kindness seems to be something we don't bother with
unless we're coerced. We are kind out of fear of being pun-
ished if we aren't kind. Whereas kindness as a desire, as something integral to what desiring is, is irresistible. Ordered to
be kind, we are likely to be cruel; wanting to be kind, we
are likely to discover our generosity. The dangers of fellow
feeling, from a psychoanalytic point of view, are therefore
twofold: First, our genuine kindness makes us unobliging,
less susceptible to moral coercion from within and without.
That is to say, by refusing the extortion of kindness, we allow

it as a pleasure. And second, once we allow it as a pleasure it makes us more porous, less insulated and separated from others. Once you put kindness back in the picture there can be no such thing as the isolated self. Because our sexual desire is far more selective than our kindness, our preconditions for excitement are much narrower than our preconditions for sympathy: we feel for more people than we desire—sexuality hives us off. Fellow feeling joins us to various and diverse other people. Kindness is extravagant.

The child is a creature of sympathetic attachments. There has always been, and will always be, conflict between the generations (and the sexes). The aggression, and the rivalry and envy and spite of children, has never been a secret, even if their sexuality has been. But it is only in the modern era that the child's tenderness, the child's natural kindness, has been so much under suspicion. (One of the forms this suspicion takes is the idealizing of children's innocence to cancel our doubts about it.) And it is in their descriptions of childhood, however scientifically framed, that modern adults have tended to play out their fears about themselves. The modern Western adult's fear about himself is that, to put it as crudely as possible, his hatred is stronger than his love; that there is, in the British psychoanalyst Ernest Jones's words, "much less love in the world than there appears to be." Our kindness is chronically in doubt (and not, as philosophical skeptics have traditionally tried to persuade us, our existence). Childhood has become the last bastion of kindess, the last place where we may find more love in the world than there appears to be.

Indeed, the modern obsession with child-rearing may be no more and no less than an obsession about the possibility of kindness in a society that makes it harder and harder to believe in kindness. Talking about child development and about parenting may be one of the only ways we have now of talking about fellow feeling.

Compassion, which all the so-called great world religions promote, and altruism, which has been proffered as a comparable secular value, have never found their place as significant terms in modern psychologies. And the apparent realism of all the self-interest stories—the accounts of human nature as essentially self-seeking and self-satisfying—have made the kindness stories sound soppy or wishful or simply the province of the religious. Modern psychoanalysis has something to say about our fear of kindness, about why fellow feeling—our imaginative capacity to identify with other people—may be the aspect of ourselves that we find the most disturbing. Man's project, Lacan said, is to escape from his desire; it may also be to escape from his kindness. How this may have come about historically was the subject of the last chapter. Now we must look at the fate of kindness in individual childhood. Our lives, from the beginning, depend upon kindness, and it is for this reason, as we shall see, that it terrorizes us.

We begin literally of a piece with another's body; we begin as part of the very body we grow out of. All the psychoanalytic stories about development describe the modern individual as having to grow out of two forms of absolute dependence, as though after the fact of biological birth there is a further birth—a psychological birth—in which over time a person establishes herself as a separate, more or less independent individual. On the one hand the child has to be weaned from her tendency toward self-reliance, from her belief that she can satisfy herself, and that everything she needs comes from herself. This is the dependence on fantasy—as though fantasy alone can nourish—which becomes, in adult life, the refuge of daydreaming. On the other hand, in the opposite direction as it were, the child has to be weaned from her absolute dependence on her mother for her survival and well-being. The child, and the adult she will become, has to renounce her wishful world of fantasy in order to be nourished by reality (imagining the meal you want may satisfy you but it won't fill you up); and she has to displace her proliferating needs onto other people apart from her mother. One way of describing this dual process (much as Rousseau described it in the maturing Emile) would be to say that it involves the growing child in extending the range of her sympathies and interests; that growing up, if anything, is the imaginative elaboration of fellow feeling: the acknowledgment that other people have what we need and that their well-being matters to us.

And yet, of course, what psychoanalysts have tended to observe and speculate about are the ways in which these developmental processes don't work, or don't work in the ways that we might want them to. The self-satisfactions of narcissism—and the consequent rejection of others and hatred of our need for them—are never entirely given up; and something about our love and desire, first for the mother, and then for the parents, is indelible, both impossible to satisfy and impossible to give up. But in order to survive we have to get to reality—to the reality of our acknowledged need for our parents as people separate from ourselves (though of the same kind); and we have to get beyond the reality of our parents in order to have a viable erotic and reproductive life. In Darwinian terms one might say: the first task is survival, which entails dependence on parental love and care; and once that is established, the next is the creation of conditions for reproduction and/or sexual satisfaction. There is the wanting of parents and then the limit set to the wanting of parents by what is called the incest taboo.

From a developmental point of view, it is not difficult to see why aspects of one's love and desire for one's parents must be renounced and transferred to others. But why should kindness itself be sacrificed in the process? From a Freudian/ Winnicottian point of view, too much kindness is a saboteur of development, of fully formed independence. From this perspective, a certain ruthlessness—a capacity to use the parents when you need them and drop them when you don't—is required in growing up. If development is seen as graduated separation from one's parents, then the kindness that is fellow feeling threatens reunion. Fellow feeling in the family can begin to seem like incest by other means; it begins to smack of regressive wishes as though feeling-for is a slippery slope toward never getting away. For the child to be too attentive, too attuned to her parents' needs at the cost of her own—and in this picture of development, one person's need is always being sacrificed, with needs oddly construed as the kind of things that can be sacrificed—is to sabotage her development. The modern child is perceived as someone who can lose the necessary momentum of development if she has too much fellow feeling for her parents. It is only if the parents consent to being treated callously—that is, without concern for their own needs—that the child can be the entrepreneur of her own growth. In this story, which is clearly part of everyone's experience in growing up, kindness is something we need, but also need to be wary of.

Every small child has to ensure that it has the parents it requires to survive and to grow up. How can the child ensure that her parents meet her needs without themselves being harmed? To do so, the child must be lovable enough to induce the parents to look after her. And this is where kindness initially comes in, as a bribe to the parents, an insurance policy against deprivation or neglect. The child wishes to save the parents from everything that makes them unhappy, from anything that might interfere with meeting her needs. The child's kindness begins as a magical rescue or cure that invariably fails. Out of this failure genuine kindness emerges; or it does if the parents can tolerate the failure. Once the child begins to realize what magical kindness cannot do—it cannot make everything all right—her real kindness can come into play. Parents who recruit the child to save themselves, who punish the child when she cannot make the world a good place for them, may destroy the child's belief in kindness. A society that romanticizes kindness, that regards it as a virtue so difficult to sustain that only the magically good can manage it, destroys people's faith in real or ordinary kindness. Supposed to make everything happy and right, magical kindness cannot deliver the realistic care and reassurance that people actually need. Magical kindness is a false promise.

Ordinary kindness is not a manipulative bribe or a magical cure, but a simple exchange. In a parent-child relationship where no one is looking to the other to rescue him, each can enjoy the other without needing to transform him. The modern child is perceived as someone who is always running the risk of having to become a parent to her parents; someone whose concern for her parents' well-being can be the very thing that waylays her developmental needs. In other words, modern stories about child development are like cries for help from the grown-ups, who sound strangely oppressed if not actually enslaved by their children. It is as if now parents are more dependent on their children than children are on their parents; that what we are left with after two hundred years of the intensive study of children is a world in which parents are frightened of their children, of their vulnerability, their neediness, their frustration, and their rage—and in which parents look to their children for so-called self-esteem, to give their lives point and purpose. In which, to put it as simply as possible, parents and children are unable to collaborate with each other in the ordinary business of growing up. Committed to magical kindness—to the avoidance of frustration at all costs—parents can only fail. For people committed to an image of the child as a bundle of rapacious, fundamentally insatiable desires, growing up becomes little more than a type of profiteering. It is this predicament that psychoanalysis seeks to address: What happens to kindness and fellow feeling in the hothouse of the family? What if anything can be done to prevent kindness becoming the first casualty of family life?

Whatever else it is, psychoanalysis is an account of how and why modern people are so frightened of each other. What Freud called defenses are the ways we protect ourselves from our desires, which are also our relations with others. Indeed, the history of psychoanalysis after Freud reflects many of the dilemmas we have about kindness (it would be an interesting exercise to read "sexuality" as Freud's word for "fellow feeling"). Are we, Freud's followers wondered, committed to our desires and their gratification, or to other people? And what, if anything, could such a distinction mean? Do we crave (sensuous) satisfaction as so-called drive theorists say, or do we crave intimacy and relationships? Do we want good company or good sex, if we have to choose? If kindness, in its anti-sentimental sense, is at the heart of human desiring, then these become merely false choices, the wrong way of talking about what goes on between people. Sex becomes one of the more complicated forms of fellow feeling (there is no sex without kindness or its refusal); and aggression becomes one of its more obscure, least articulated forms (there is no kindness without aggression or its refusal). It is kind not to overprotect other people from oneself, especially from one's sexuality.

The eroticization of kindness in the psychoanalytic account was not entirely new. Rousseau, as we have seen, located the psychological birth of kindness in the onset of puberty. It is sexual maturation that opens the fictional Emile to the feelings and sufferings of others, "bring[ing] to his heart the first compassion it has ever experienced." But erotic desire, as the adult Emile soon discovers, is conflict-ridden, as likely to give rise to animosity as to *pitié*. As Rousseau intimated, and Freud showed so clearly, ambivalence is key to human sexuality; and if there is one thing that clearly exposes this ambivalence, and tests human kindness, it is the experience of sexual jealousy. Indeed, the most interesting, the most disturbing thing that the adult experience of sexual jealousy exposes is just how precarious our kindness is. The fate of kindness in sexual jealousy—the undoing of generosity in betrayal—is a vital clue: the danger of kindness is in its undoing, in what we lose, in how we have to live, when kindness is no longer possible.

The ambivalence exposed so vividly by sexual jealousy— that where we love we always hate, and vice versa—has something important to tell us about the complexity of our emotional lives. If such extreme, apparently opposed feelings are always present—why else would we hate if love wasn't somewhere involved? You can be frustrated only by someone you need—then we need to be attentive when these strong feelings seem to be mutually exclusive, when love takes over so you can't find the hate, and vice versa. We are always tempted to simplify our emotional lives in order to diminish the constant conflict we are in; in sexual jealousy we can no longer keep our conflicts hidden. We hate intensely where we once loved; our dependence on the person we need, and our inability to control their desire, is unavoidably disclosed to us. Indeed, the experience of sexual jealousy—the ambivalence that explodes out of it—invites us to ask our question the other way round: Why are we ever unkind? And one answer would be, to secure, insofar as it is possible, our emotional (psychic) survival. The fundamental threat to our survival is, for want of a better way of putting it, loss of love, the threatened or actual loss of what our lives depend upon, which begins most urgently in childhood. The small child lives in the illusion that he controls the mother, the person he needs, and that she has no desires of her own that exclude him. His kindness *is* this illusion. The dawning awareness of the mother's independence and the loss of the child's picture of himself as omnipotent engenders rage. Much of our cruelty is the largely unsuccessful attempt to restore or to recover the state of things before this catastrophic disillusionment. And this perhaps is why sexual jealousy has haunted the Western imagination: it puts our kindness, our original link to other people, under threat. We are at our most merciless, to ourselves and to others, when we are sexually jealous. In love and affection kindness is experienced as a desire rather than a duty, and one of the things that psychoanalysis does, as we shall see, is to give us ways of describing this difference. Sexual jealousy always runs the risk of being the death or even the murder of kindness. (In *Othello*, for example, it is both.) The horror of it, in other words, is not only the loss of the loved person, it is the loss of the individual's capacity for kindness. The origins of self-hatred are often to be found in failures of kindness.

In a lecture on sexual jealousy delivered in Paris in 1929, Ernest Jones argued that what we call love is very often simply the way we manage our hatred. By then the idea that hate was stronger than love was old hat, at least in psychoanalytic circles and, of course, not only in psychoanalytic circles after the cataclysm of the First World War. If love was innate, if the infant was born with a capacity for love which was tantamount to a capacity for survival, this love was sure to be frustrated, which in turn would unleash a whirlwind of fury or a slump of sulking (what Jones described prosaically as the "resentment" consequent on disappointment "at the love not proving the perfect ideal they had imagined and expected"). If hatred was as innate as love, as Freud would begin to believe, then hatred seemed to be the stronger of the two. In love we are likely to be fighting a losing battle; or, to put it rather differently, love never seems to deliver exactly what we want it to. Love never works as magic, but it can work as kindness.

Freud described the ambivalence that, in his view, constituted human nature in a way that made original sin sound like the kind of idea people would come up with if they didn't know about psychoanalysis. There was something about us, something about how we loved, that tended to destroy the very things we valued most. We were, as Freud among many others had noticed, more destructive, more violent than we wanted to be; but also, as Freud and so many others had also noticed, less destructive, less violent than we were inclined to be. We could live only by inhibiting our aggression, but inhibiting our aggression made us sick (inhibited aggression, like inhibited kindness, can feel like self-betrayal). And the story Freud told about modern human development put violent hatred and sexual desire, in that order, as the main protagonists. If chance determined our fate, our primal passions did everything within their range to satisfy themselves. But hatred was the first thing, the preeminent thing, which love could, if we were lucky, help us to recover from. There was, in Freud's view, an original hatred that owed nothing to God.

In *Drives and Their Fates*, written in 1915, a year into World War I, Freud wrote:

> As an object relation, hate is older than love, its source being the narcissistic ego's primal rejection of the stimuli of the outside world. As an expression of the reaction of unpleasure provoked by objects, it remains forever closely related to the self-preservation drives, so that ego-drives and sexual-drives readily form an opposition replicating that between hate and love.

The complicated Freudian jargon has a simple picture in it, but one with perhaps startling implications. What we call hatred is our rejection of everything in the external world that doesn't work for us, that endangers our well-being. The good things we take for granted—the loving comforts, the satisfactions, the protection—but the bad things have to be warded off in the service of self-preservation. Hatred is our primal form of self-protection, a closing off from everything that threatens us. Our sexuality, which Freud equates with our love, opens us up to the satisfactions we can't find in ourselves.

There are always, according to Freud, "frequent conflicts between self-interest and love interests." We reach out to others for love and in the process we come up against things that disturb us. At its most extreme, the paradox Freud proposes is that we would rather starve than risk our lives; that the dangers of loving are in excess of its satisfactions. In this, as in many other things, Freud is a stalwart Darwinian: first there is the struggle for survival (both physical and emotional survival), and then, if there is sufficient safety—if psychic survival is guaranteed—there is the possibility of satisfaction from and with others. Hatred is one of our methods of survival. What Freud calls the "admixture of hate [in love] can be traced back to a source in the self-preservation drives." In love we are more preoccupied with our survival than with anything else. In this picture hatred is not, then, a sign of malevolence (innate or not), but a sign of danger. What might look like a secular version of original sin in Freud is more akin to original self-preservation. Freud was to discover that the ways we protect ourselves tend also to be the ways we imprison ourselves. Our sexuality endangers us because it turns us toward others, and that very exposure of appetite makes us vulnerable. (When it comes to appetite, all exposure is experienced as overexposure.) All animals suffer from where their appetites lead them.

Ten years later, in a paper entitled "Negation," Freud was to say all this more simply. Our lives can be understood through two straightforward questions: What do we want to take in? And what do we want to expel? What do we want to include in our lives, and who do we want to keep at a safe distance? Ideally what we take in will be what we think of as good, valuable, and necessary; what we reject will be bad, redundant, and irrelevant. Love is what we call the taking in; hatred is the expulsion. So, ironically, our so-called hatred keeps us good and keeps us going. The decision, Freud writes, for the infant as for the adult, is

> expressed in the language of the most archaic oral impulses: "I want to eat this, or spit this out." . . . That is: "I want it inside me or outside me" . . . the primal pleasure-ego wants to introject into itself everything good and expel from itself everything bad. That which is bad, that which is alien to the ego, that which is outside, are initially identical as far as it is concerned.

So the question for us is always: Who do we want to reject, or who do we want to hold onto? Which feelings do we want to dispense with and which do we enjoy?

What Freud calls the primal pleasure-ego, and we might call our original and ordinary sense of ourselves, wants to sustain our well-being and expel everything that undoes it. Things that disturb this ego, things it doesn't like, are spit out, ejected into the outside world, so the outside is what is hated. (The other place this ego puts anything that disturbs it is inside, and this is what Freud called "repression.") We like what likes us. Hatred is both our means of sustaining our pleasure and a pleasure in itself. If we can't hate we can't be happy.

We hate, in Freud's view, because we are pleasure-seeking animals; but we also, in another equally important strand of the Freudian story, get pleasure from our hatred (or make our hatred bearable by making it pleasurable). Indeed our sexual satisfaction to some extent always depends upon our capacity for sadism, for getting pleasure from our cruelty. Clearly the idea of a hatred required for self-preservation is more palatable to us, however uneasy it may make us feel, than the notion that cruelty may be integral to our essential pleasures, whether it be cruelty to ourselves or to others, or both. If Freud never ceases to be dispirited by just how much we torment ourselves, by our predilection for guilt—and to a lesser extent for shame—he is also bemused by the pervasive sadomasochism in modern sexual relations. The pleasures of cruelty and the cruelty of pleasures are famously Freud's touchstones of modern life. And broadly speaking, he has two stories about this. In one story, which is revisited and revised throughout his work, sadism is innate, almost natural— almost because he does not find it in the sexual lives of other animals, so making it appear an artifact of human instinct, something human beings have added on for reasons of survival. In the early *Three Essays on the Theory of Sexuality* (1905), sadism and masochism are what Freud calls component instincts of infantile sexuality, inevitable components in the unfolding of the individual's erotic life. In his second story, in his later mythology, all cruelties are part of what he calls the death instinct. In both versions, sadism is innate, genetically determined, as it were; each individual is born with different amounts. The individual's struggle is to make his cruelty sufficiently compatible with his so-called relationships. If, to whatever degree, he gets sexual pleasure from making other people suffer, he needs someone to do this with. The sadist, in a sense, needs to look after his masochistic partner, because he needs this partner to be sufficiently alive to his cruelty. The sadist says, "I can do what I like to you because I know you can never leave me." The masochist says, "You can do what you like to me as long as you never leave me." (Sado-masochism is the religion of those who believe you have to be cruel to be kind.) Whether destructive aggression is a response to frustration (a frustration that in the Freudian picture is integral to human relations), or whether this aggression is just one of our innate instincts (we are animals that relish or just require the doing of harm), either way it is a grim picture. In most relationships now, people are very often dismayed and confounded by the sheer scale of frustration and hostility that has to be borne. This is what Freud's story is about.

Thus, just as psychoanalysis has a developmental story about how we bear our destructive aggression—our proneness to envy, spite, and retaliation—it also has an equally compelling account of how and why we can so severely defend ourselves against too much involvement, too much feeling for both the pleasures and the sufferings of people other than ourselves. We develop an immune system to the suffering of others. For some people, their dependence on their parents when they were children was so unbearable that it can never be risked again. Concern for parents felt like self-annihilation and brought them up against the limits of what their love could do. Every child wants to cure his parents of whatever makes them unhappy, and every child fails at this. That experience alone can make the child begin to doubt the value of his kindness, because it isn't magic. Yet all people experience—almost instinctively—some degree of fellow feeling for others, and this basic kindness is very important to us, however ineffectual it may feel at times. Indeed, it can seem like a lifeline.

In the mid-eighteenth century Jean-Jacques Rousseau portrayed kindness and desire as knotted together in ways that made each necessary to the other. One hundred and fifty years later Freud likewise described kindness in erotic terms, but in ways that made kindness seem peculiarly difficult. The image of human nature developed by early Freudians made it impossible for them to put kindness on a par with sexuality, self-preservation, aggression, and life-or-death instincts. And yet the issue of fellow feeling—of what holds people together and what keeps people together—is everywhere in psychoanalysis. What it is in ourselves that resists our own kindness and the kindness of others is at the heart of psychoanalytic practice and inquiry. It later became evident to some psychoanalysts that only by taking sexuality and aggression seriously could one begin to take kindness seriously (that is, without sentimentalizing it). But this recognition was in itself very troubling. How troubling, and the consequences of this for a psychoanalytic understanding of kindness, are the subjects of the next chapter.

IV

The Kindness Instinct

Being kind always makes us feel better, and yet being kind is not something we do as often as we would like. If sexuality exposes just how divided we are against ourselves—that when it comes to sex our preferences don't always accord with our standards, that we often most want what we will most regret—kindness seems to make our contradictoriness even more confusing. There are, after all, risks in sex, in following our desire, and risk, by definition, is always an opportunity to harm oneself. We describe our erotic life in terms of temptation, of secrecy, of jealousy and betrayal and punishment. Because sexuality is so often about the forbidden, about transgression, it is never to be taken seriously as a conflict-free area of our lives. But there does, on the face of it, seem to be something strange about the idea that we could be inhibited about kindness. We are wary of our kindness as though there are risks attached to it, as though it is a kind of temptation; as though, in short, when we are being kind, we are endangering ourselves with other people—as indeed we are.

There would, of course, be an obvious, crude, but nonetheless tempting Freudian interpretation of this: that kindness, in actuality, is a polite word for seduction. That we tell ourselves we are being kind as a cover story for the trade in sex that is always going on when we think we are at our most virtuous. This may often in a certain sense be the case: and yet it is too crude a view of kindness because it is too crude a view of sex. Once again it puts the cart before the horse: because it is assumed—by Social Darwinians and Freudians alike—that we are by nature rapacious and exploitative creatures, we are then obliged to find the cruelty seething in the nice people, as though whenever sex is involved we are inevitably up to no good. It is not that kindness needs to be saved from its connection with sex, but rather that sex needs to be redescribed in a way that makes kindness less obscure. For example, if people are too kind—too thoughtful, too considerate, too sensitive—sex can be insufficiently exciting; if they are not kind enough, it can be too frightening to enjoy.

And this is where psychoanalysis comes in, not as the ultimate arbiter of the real truth about sex and kindness but as a way of accounting for human behavior that emerges at a time when older, more religious ways of thinking about kindness are being displaced by newer, "scientific" modes of thought.

If the religious question is: How can people created by a good God do cruel things? then the secular question taken up by psychoanalysts is: Why should the human animal, created by no deity, driven by sex and survival, be kind? In what sense is kindness compatible with the sexuality that seems to be in our nature and with the modern forms of political and economic organization through which we survive? Psychoanalysis developed as a set of stories about the casualties of modern life, about "neurotics," for whom appetite and fellow feeling had become incompatible. And what these stories kept saying in all their singularity and in all their myriad forms is that sexuality is a problem because it can be so starkly at odds with our capacity for kindness. Sexuality only becomes a problem if we care about ourselves and others.

The story Freud and his followers had to tell about child development as sexual development was not likely to endear them to their contemporaries. The violence of children would hardly have been news: any child's tantrum, or visit to a local playground, would serve as an easy reminder of the aggressive mayhem of the very young. But to redescribe this violence, as Freud did in the first instance, as sexual behavior was illuminating when it wasn't too shocking. To suggest, as Freud would later do in his continual revision of his work, that our lives are a battleground between two mythical forces, a life instinct and a death instinct, and that sexuality is recruitable by both, was just another way of talking about what stopped people getting on with themselves and others; and, indeed, what might stop them wanting to. What, in other words, people's desire for and pleasure in fellow feeling was competing with. There is not going to be any consensus inside us about what we want and what we need; there is only going to be a coexistence of competing claims, the conflict of rival pleasures. What, Freud was using psychoanalysis to wonder, did kindness endanger in ourselves? What was it in conflict with? Did it make any sense to think that there might be even an instinct, or a drive for kindness, akin to or a part of a sexual instinct? When Freud defines Eros, the life instinct, as aiming "to establish ever greater unities [within and between people], and to preserve them thus—in short, to bind together," and the so-called death instinct as aiming, "on the contrary, to undo connections, and so to destroy things," it is difficult to imagine kindness as something that undoes connections and destroys things. And as a shorthand definition of fellow feeling, establishing and preserving ever greater unities between people would seem to be more than adequate. Yet Freud and his followers could never quite conceive of this as a kindness instinct.

The issue of fellow feeling is everywhere in psychoanalysis, which over time became the site for people's abiding concern with their capacity for kindness. People first came (and continue to come) to psychoanalysis not simply because they were more unhappy, especially sexually unhappy, than they could bear, but because they were not able to be as kind as they wanted to be. Something, one could say, had gone wrong with their fellow feeling for themselves and others, and it was highlighted in their erotic lives. Their sexuality was a picture of their sociability: "Tell me how someone makes love," Freud was reputed to have said to the Hungarian analyst Sándor Ferenczi, "and I will tell you everything about their character."

Freud concludes the first of his revolutionary *Three Essays on the Theory of Sexuality* of 1905 with a simple but still quite startling assertion:

> We have been in the habit of regarding the connection between the sexual instinct and the sexual object as more intimate than it in fact is. Experience of the cases that are considered abnormal has shown us that in them the sexual instinct and the sexual object are merely soldered together—a fact which we have been in danger of overlooking in consequence of the uniformity of the normal picture, where the object appears to form part and parcel of the instinct. We are thus warned to loosen the bond that exists in our thoughts between instinct and object; nor is its origin likely to be due to the object's attractions.

Freud is saying two things here. First, that the abnormal, in this case the sexually abnormal, is the key to understanding the normal; that the normal, in a sense, is a version of the abnormal. And second, that when it comes to sexuality the "normal picture" conceals something disturbing that threatens to undermine our most cherished assumptions about romance and desire. We may think we love someone because they are extraordinary (to us), but in fact, Freud suggests, they are extraordinary because we love them. Our experience may be that particular people, or even "types," call up our desire, but it is our satisfaction that we are in search of; what Freud calls the "object's attractions" are secondary. It is our desire and its satisfaction that attracts us, not its objects. It is our wanting that we are wedded to. This puts the other person, the object of our desire, in a strange position. The person who might seem most essential to us becomes the person who is most replaceable. We are attached, Freud wants us to see, to our own gratification, but not, therefore, primarily to other people.

If the object is "soldered" on to the instinct then it is at once artificial and forced; something manmade rather than automatic, contrived rather than natural (Freud uses "soldered" six times in his voluminous writings, three times with the prefix "merely"). It is as though, Freud suggests, in our attempt to understand our perplexing sexuality we have been looking in the wrong place, as though we imagined we could find out about our desire simply by looking at what we desire. This would be like believing that we could understand how the eye works by noticing what it looked at, or that studying a football could tell us how to kick it.

So important was this new idea for Freud that in 1910 he added a footnote to this essay that both explained it and gave it, supposedly, some historical grounding. "The most striking distinction between the erotic life of antiquity and our own no doubt lies in the fact," he writes, "that the ancients laid the stress on the instinct itself, whereas we emphasize its object. The ancients glorified the instinct and were prepared on its account to honor even an inferior object; while we despise the instinctual activity itself, and find excuses for it only in the merits of the object." There is little historical evidence for this, but it is indeed a striking idea; perhaps we are more in love with our desire than we are with other people.

For modern people, Freud is saying, there has been a turning away from valuing the sexual instinct; the only way modern people can justify their sexual desire is to privilege its object ("her great beauty/character/wealth, etc., prove that my desire is good: only a good thing would want a good thing"). But if you value the instinct over the object, as Freud says the ancients did, you do not have to believe that your instinct does the object good. It makes them good, that is, desirable, but it isn't necessarily good *for* them. In being committed to your satisfaction you are not necessarily committed to the well-being of the object who satisfies you; and if you *are* concerned, you are concerned merely to sustain that person as a gratifying object for you. Your kindness would ultimately be akin to the kindness of the sadist who needs to keep his masochistic partner alive so he can go on torturing him. What Freud's distinctions between the sexually normal and the abnormal, between the ancients and the moderns, describe is how other people matter to us, the nature of our concern for both others and ourselves. In Freud's picture, instrumental kindness makes sense: we are kind to the objects of our desire in the hope that they will go on satisfying us. In Freud's community of solitary, desiring individuals attached "in the first instance" to their instincts, kindness is a bribe. Kindness is foreplay. Freud, in other words, was asking himself something that his followers would try to answer: in the new method of describing (modern) people that was psychoanalysis, how, if at all, did kindness fit in? What versions of kindness were possible, of kindness to oneself and other people, in an instinct-driven world rather than a providential one?

"Kindness" is not a word Freud uses in *Three Essays on the Theory of Sexuality*. But this in itself might give us pause, given the problem of sexuality. The difficulties that modern people have with sexual desire are always, in one way or another, connected to the harm it does. When it comes to their sexuality, modern people, in Freud's view, are always caught between their safety and their excitement, between their wishes for satisfaction and their fear of guilt. (Guilt being the cruelty, the extreme unkindness, one is capable of doing to oneself.) It is, in fact, impossible to talk about sexuality without talking more or less about kindness; and yet this is what Freud almost manages to do in *Three Essays*. When the sexual instinct, as he puts it, "is subordinated to the reproductive function it becomes, so to say, altruistic," otherwise it is simply about the gratification of innate desire. What is striking for Freud is that modern human sexuality seems to have cut loose from the other animal sexualities; that the human animal doesn't have sex solely for the sake of the species and its perpetuation; she doesn't subordinate the sexual instinct to its reproductive function. Her sexuality is described as having competing projects. The implication is clear: sexuality is not something done primarily for the good of others or with others particularly in mind. What we share in this picture, what we have in common, is a primary commitment to our own instinctual satisfaction. (In this context it would be kind, presumably, just to acknowledge this.) Why should people care about each other, be concerned for each other's well-being or mindful of each other's preoccupations, except as a way of ensuring that they will be available for gratification when it is needed? In this stark picture, other people exist for the individual only insofar as they are the means, the instruments, of his own gratification. They have no significance other than the possibilities for satisfaction that they provide. Other people are there to populate our masturbation fantasies.

Modern sexuality as described by Freud has become unmoored from its reproductive function and is transgressive in its intent. Freud employs the Oedipus myth to show that the modern individual is not merely half-hearted about reproducing the species, but that his deepest desire is not to; the Freudian child wants to possess the parent of the opposite sex and to remove the parent of the same sex (and vice versa). It is the forbidden satisfaction that she seeks. If child rearing is no longer integral to sexual relations, and sexual relations are constituted by the desire for forbidden (incestuous) pleasure, then what, if anything, is going to hold people together? The question, as the world moved inexorably toward the Second World War, became urgent. At a time when hate and aggression were becoming ascendant, what was left of the kindness of humankind? How were the bonds of human fellowship to survive, and did it matter if they didn't? War with a "foreign" enemy—as many psychoanalysts were to remark—can make it easier to be kind to one's compatriots. You can be kind to someone, these psychoanalysts assumed, only if you have someone else, preferably someone far away, to hate. Kindness and hatred were seen as mutually exclusive.

The most fundamental tie—one that could easily be taken to be the source if not the blueprint for all human bonds—is the one between mother and child. This, at least, was the presumption of the psychoanalytic profession after the world wars: that nothing less than the future of Western civilization might depend upon understanding what went on between mothers and their infants, especially what could go wrong between them. Out of their work with evacuated children during the Second World War, Anna Freud, Melanie Klein, John Bowlby, and Donald Winnicott evolved their complementary and competing theories about the essentials of child development. Whatever else warfare is about, it is about separation, vulnerability, and aggression, and these were to be at the heart of this pioneering new work on the needs of children and the needs of adults in relation to children. This postwar generation of psychoanalysts believed that it was no longer sexual relations between adults that was the key to a useful understanding of modern human nature, but child rearing. The adult's remembered, re-created childhood—the childhood reconstructed in psychoanalytic treatment—was no longer sufficiently telling. What was needed was a more direct, empirical study of childhood itself. The psychoanalysis of children rather than the psychoanalysis of adults in recovery from their childhoods seemed to be the most promising future for psychoanalytic research. Mothers and breasts and babies began to take center stage, with genitals and fathers consigned to the wings. The stark titles of John Bowlby's classic trilogy more or less tell the story: *Attachment* (1969), *Separation* (1973), and *Loss* (1980). After the devastations of the world wars there was more to be said, at least in Britain, about aggression and depression and mourning than about sexual excitement.

By preferring the mother–child couple to the adult sexual couple, the postwar psychoanalysts were, among other things, privileging kindness over desire; and this, as we shall see, was a mixed blessing. (It was the British, and later the Americans, who privileged mothers and babies in their theorizing; the French kept faith with sexuality.) Kindness, in this context, became an odd, rather old-fashioned blend of a natural, largely maternal instinct with a moral imperative. It was never updated in psychoanalysis in the way that erotic relations were. Sexual desire, Freud and his early followers had suggested, could be sabotaged by kindness, but no one wanted to talk about the mother's unkindness and its effect on the child's development. If (some) adults needed to inhibit their kindness and concern for others in order to fully satisfy themselves, it was less easy to see what kind of problem kindness might be between mothers and children. Whereas the sexual adult, from a psychoanalytic point of view, needed to resist at least the excesses of his own kindness in order to desire, it was the difficulties of being kind that needed to be understood in the nursing couple: the mother's so-called failures of empathy and identification and the child's aggression that precluded his being nurtured. If both mother and baby were ambivalent about each other, what was the fate of kindness in this first and formative relationship?

In short, the kindness that was traditionally taken for granted between mothers and their babies became part of the problem of adult sexuality. The mother–child couple had to be sufficiently kind to each other for development to take place; the adult sexual couple had to be sufficiently unkind for gratification to be possible. The adult, in Freud's original picture, wants to satisfy herself; the child, in the new postwar psychoanalytic picture, wants to develop. They are quite different projects. And one of the ways of teasing out this difference is to see the work kindness is supposed to be doing. It is kindness that makes us grow, insisted post-Freudian British psychoanalysts (often referred to as object relations theorists), and growing up is what we want to do. But from the Freudian perspective, kindness is the very thing that can make our sexuality an impossible conflict.

This is the paradox that psychoanalysis presents us with. It is a symptomatic profession in the sense that it exposes our muddles and our conflicts about kindness. If our early life depends upon the very thing that can undermine our sexuality, and our sexuality is the very thing that makes our adult life worth living, we are truly divided against ourselves. Is kindness the solution or the problem? For psychoanalysis, kindness became the conundrum in human development. So it is to the boon and the bane of kindness, as described by psychoanalysis, that we need now to turn. And we can do this best by briefly comparing two famous psychoanalytic essays, Freud's 1912 paper instructively titled "On the Universal Tendency to Debasement in the Sphere of Love," and Winnicott's 1947 paper "Hate in the Countertransference."

If Freud had called his paper "On the Tendency to Debasement in the Sphere of Love," the reader might have assumed that only certain people—possibly a diagnostic category of people—were prone to such distasteful behavior. A "universal" tendency, on the other hand, appears to be part of human nature. Something that we might have hoped was the province of a few "perverts," Freud implies, belongs to all of us. We may all want to kill the thing we love, but most of us don't actually do it; we may all want to debase the thing we love, and this may be actually what we do need to do, in order to love. All of us some of the time and some of us all the time can love—in the full sexual sense of desiring and consummating our desire—only if we can treat the loved one badly. Unkindness, lack of regard and of consideration, is a precondition for what Freud refers to in this paper as "psychical potency" in love, and what we can call, more simply, the capacity for real satisfaction in love. As a scientist Freud has a cause-and-effect story to tell us, and as a writer he manages to evoke in his reader considerable unease as romance becomes degradation, and care becomes the enemy of excitement.

"It sounds not only disagreeable but paradoxical," Freud writes—and the reader is unlikely to disagree—"yet it must nevertheless be said that anyone who is to be really happy and free in love must have surmounted his respect for women and must have come to terms with the idea of incest with his mother or sister." We need to know what such surmountings involve, and what terms we might be able to come to. But the story Freud has to tell is a simple one, where our route into understanding so-called normal sexuality is through pathology. The extremes of human sexual behavior shed light on normal development. Analyzing "psychical impotence" in men—"men of strong libidinous natures . . . [with] a refusal by the executive organs of sexuality to carry out the sexual act"—Freud discovers that "the foundation of the disorder" can be found in the history of the individual's sexual development. "Two currents," he writes, "whose union is necessary to ensure a completely normal attitude in love have, in the cases we are considering, failed to combine. These two may by distinguished as the affectionate and the sensual current." We have to imagine that there are two versions of ourselves, two animating forces in our development. One, which Freud calls "the affectionate current," is the "older of the two [and] springs from the earliest years of childhood" (so that we might call it a natural disposition). The affectionate side of our nature comes, he says, from "the self-preservative instinct" and it is the basis, the medium, of our relations with our families, with the first people who love and care for us. This affection "carries along with it," as Freud puts it, "contributions from the sexual instinct," as does our parents' affection for us. So whenever as adults we desire someone, this very desire links us again to our first, forbidden, incestuous objects of desire. At puberty the "affectionate fixations" of the child for the family "are joined by the powerful sensual current which no longer mistakes its aims." Our sexual, sensual desire as adolescents and adults is guided by the affectionate desires of childhood. If we have sexual relations with people for whom we feel affection, it is as though, in our unconscious, so to speak, we are committing incest. So we do something that psychoanalysts call "splitting": there are people we feel affection for, and there are people with whom we have sex, and ne'er the twain shall meet.

For those people for whom this anxiety is particularly acute—and Freud, of course, implies that this is all of us—

there is a determined, though often unwitting, avoidance of certain people, usually the people we most desire. "A restriction has thus been placed on object-choice," Freud writes in his sober quasi-scientific prose.

> The sensual current that has remained active seeks only objects which do not recall the incestuous figures forbidden to it; if someone makes an impression that might lead to a high physical estimation for her, this impression does not find an issue in any sensual excitation but in affection which has no erotic effect. The whole sphere of love in such people remains divided in the two directions personified in art as sacred and profane (or animal) love. Where they love they do not desire and where they desire they cannot love.

We begin, Freud suggests, with something akin to a kindness instinct that he calls variously a "self-preservative instinct" and an "affectionate current." We have these feelings for our parents, as they do for us, but a sexual "sensual" instinct gets mixed in with this affection (Freud's image for the prototype of sexual satisfaction is the infant satiated at the mother's breast). By nature we associate affection with desire; by culture—the incest taboo—we have to break that association. The self-cure for this ineradicable ("universal") conflict that renders men impotent, beyond sexual satisfaction, is what Freud calls "debasement." "The main protective measure against such a disturbance which men have recourse to in this split in their love consists in a physical debasement of the sexual object, the overvaluation that normally attaches to the sexual object being reserved for the incestuous object and its representatives."

We know someone is reminding us of our parents, Freud says, because we find ourselves idealizing them, or "overvaluing" them, as he puts it more suggestively. They are the people whom we mustn't have sex with. Indeed, the only people we are free to desire are those who are as far as possible from being idealizable. In order to have sex we either choose "degraded" objects—people well below our standards of what is appropriate—or, more often, we degrade them ourselves in order to render them desirable. It is as if we can enjoy people only by treating them badly. It is our unkindness—our lack of affection and regard—that makes our desire possible; kindness is the way we stop ourselves desiring. (In childhood, we should remember, kindness is the medium of appetite and relating.) When we are being kind we know we are dealing with forbidden objects; kindness is what children and parents do with each other; sex is what parents and children must not do with each other. We associate kindness with frustration; unkindness with satisfaction. If we are to be sexually satisfied adults we have to learn to be unkind, to bear our unkindness. Sexual pleasure, along the Freudian lines, is a ruthless business.

Freud, as perhaps one might expect, is rather more reticent in this paper about women. He was always, quite rightly, skeptical about himself as a man talking on behalf of women and their wants. It was, of course, a logical implication of his paper, though not spelled out by him, that any sexual encounter that is unsatisfying for one person must, in a sense, be unsatisfying for the other; the undegradable woman is going to have a very frustrated and resentful man on her hands. But Freud is keener to say that because "civilization" holds women back from sexual knowledge and sexual experience for so long in their development, it is harder for women to "undo the connection between sensual activity and the prohibition [of incest]." It is as though for women, in Freud's view, sexual life is lived so long in fantasy that they are out of practice. They are, however, as subject to the incest taboo as men are, and so have a comparable problem: in their minds for a very long time they have connected love and desire, but in reality they will have to eventually separate them. They do this, Freud suggests, through secrecy, through the furtiveness of their lusts. "The condition of forbiddenness in the erotic life of women is, I think, comparable to the need on the part of men to debase their sexual object. . . . Both aim at abolishing the physical impotence that results from the failure of affectionate and sensual impulses to coalesce."

In order to desire, men debase women; in order to desire, women keep their own desires secret (even from themselves). The kindness of childhood—upon which parenting depends—makes a problem of desire in adulthood. Affection is inevitably entwined with strong feelings for parents; it becomes a nice word for incest. Kindness and prohibition are inextricable; kindness is our recognition of the forbidden and our refusal of it. This is the paradox Freud presents us with. It is the nature of our sexuality that makes kindness more of a problem than it might seem. There is, Freud implies, though he never says it like this, a kindness instinct, but it quickly becomes part and parcel of a sexual instinct that in human beings is essentially transgressive. Because of the incest taboo our desire is experienced as a risk. Our kindness, in other words, is the key to our sexual problems, and not the other way round. Freud never confronted the obvious questions: How can the individual render his kindness of a piece with his desire? What is it to be sexually kind, if sexually kind means sexually satisfied? Mothers, clearly, must not debase their children in order to love them, but adults have a tendency to debasement in the sphere of love.

If anything was to signify the modern horrors of coexistence it was the two world wars. Psychoanalysis is of its time in its obsession with conflict and the impossibilities of modern relationships. The improbability of harmony between the sexes and generations, as between modern nation states, haunts everything that Freud wrote. So it is not surprising in this context that kindness fell under suspicion. If there was to be a viable modern kindness, the psychoanalysts had begun to believe, it had to be allied to aggression, it had to possess a more forceful vitality; it couldn't be a wishful refuge from the patent brutality of human nature. The kindness of Christian humility had begun to seem, from a psychoanalytic point of view, very suspect. Freud had said, before the First World War, that kindness split off from sexual desire breeds a fundamental frustration which in turn leads to a destructive hatred that, directed against the self, becomes impotence and frigidity. Winnicott was to say, in a paper written at the end of the Second World War, that the child can only "believe in being loved after reaching being hated"; kindness split from hatred breeds a fundamental loss of contact with oneself and others that leads to a prevailing feeling of unreality, or being unrecognized. There could be no intimacy without hatred, and no enduring pleasurable contact between people without surviving the hatred that always exists in relationships.

In "Hate in the Countertransference" Winnicott picks a group of patients he calls psychotics—just as Freud had selected a group of patients suffering from "psychic impotence"—to say something more general; as if it were only in the extreme cases that we can see ourselves for what we are. Winnicott's so-called psychotics are different from neurotics in one essential way: neurotics, Winnicott says, know the difference between love and hate and expect themselves and others to be ambivalent; they will take it for granted, in other words, that in human relationships—and in one's relationships with oneself—there will be the continual to-and-fro of loving and hating feelings (I will love someone when they please me and hate them when they withdraw their pleasures).

The psychotics—who, in Winnicott's view, are developmentally deprived—live at what is taken to be a more primitive, earlier level, akin to that of an infant without a reliable mother. For these people, love and hate always come together, at exactly the same time, and this is extremely disturbing. When these people seek psychoanalysis they re-create this terrifying situation with the analyst, and this creates problems (the patient will presume, for example, that "should the analyst show love, he will surely at the same moment kill the patient"). We do not need to go into the psychoanalytic intricacies of this to get to Winnicott's point, which, like all the most interesting points in psychoanalysis, is extremely simple and simply illustrated. "It is perhaps relevant here," Winnicott writes by way of illustration, "to cite the case of the child of the broken home, or the child without parents. Such a child spends his time unconsciously looking for his parents. It is notoriously inadequate to take such a child into one's home and love him. What happens is that after a while a child so adopted gains hope, and then he starts to test out the environment that he has found, and to seek proof of his guardian's ability to hate objectively. It seems that he can believe in being loved only after reaching being hated."

This simple and vivid example is informed both by Winnicott's work during the war with evacuated children and by his psychoanalytic work with psychotic adults (psychotics in this sense are like children who have been evacuated from somewhere that never felt like home). If the adopted child is loved without having been hated, then, from the child's point of view, his nature is not known; it is as though he were only capable of being loved by people who don't want to recognize who he is, and what he is capable of. Those who love without hating cannot be believed in, cannot be trusted. Kindness entails the acknowledgment of hatred. It is kind to see people as they are and not as one would like them to be.

We described in the last chapter the journey taken by the small child from magical kindness—kindness as a love bribe to his parents, a rescue from and cure of all that troubles them, and that might interfere with their caretaking of him—to genuine kindness, which can accommodate hostility and aggression. The thing that works, Winnicott says—the thing that makes relations between parents and children "feel real," in his phrase—is the hatred that is lived through without severing the relationship. In Winnicott's preferred developmental story, it is only through hatred that relations between people move out of fantasy and into reality, into the possibility of actual exchange. And this is for a simple reason: hatred is what the child feels when he can let himself acknowledge that the parent (inevitably) frustrates him; that the parent is not the ideal, all-giving, ever-present figure in his mind but a real person (it is not the real mother who has limitations, it is the idealized mother who cannot actually nourish the child). It is only when we compare real people with the men or women of our dreams that they disappoint. In Winnicott's view, once the child has felt and lived out his frustration with the real mother and father, and they have survived it—which might involve hating the child back but without in any way abandoning him—he can resume his relationship with them more realistically; he has added to the stock of available reality. If he had turned away from them at this point—retreated from real engagement, stopped making demands—or they had turned away from him, they would all have gone on living a fantasy life together (ideal relations as an enraged retreat from real life). Real kindness, real fellow feeling, entails hating and being hated—that is, really feeling available frustrations—and through this, coming to a more realistic relationship. This, one might say, is a more robust version of kindness, a kindness made possible through frustration and hatred rather than a kindness organized to repudiate (or to disown) such feelings. Kindness of this variety allows for ambivalence and conflict while false, or magical, kindness distorts our perceptions of other people, often by sentimentalizing them, to avoid conflict. Sentimentality is cruelty by other means.

Winnicott concludes his paper with a point that is, in its way, as transgressive as it is obvious: "I suggest that the mother hates the baby before the baby hates the mother, and before the baby can know his mother hates him." And he then lists eighteen very good reasons why a mother would hate her baby: "He is ruthless, treats her as scum, an unpaid servant, a slave. . . . The baby is an interference with her private life, a challenge to preoccupation. . . . If she fails him at the start she knows he will pay her out for ever. . . . He excited her but frustrated her—she mustn't eat him or trade in sex with him," and so on.

We have all been the objects of hatred, but it is hatred denied or refused that for Winnicott is the problem for both mother and child. Right from the beginning we have been hateful without knowing it; our mothers have had to hold this very difficult line between feeling this inevitable hatred and protecting the child from feeling too much of it. This is the trauma of motherhood, the containment of excessive hatred, the living out of excessive love. But the real bond, Winnicott insists, has to include hatred. Without felt hatred—without the acknowledgment of harm and frustration as integral to human relations—kindness becomes a protection racket, fellow feeling becomes a denial of the feelings actually held in common.

For Winnicott, following Freud, the project with regard to kindness is to describe those forms of kindness that are not obstacles to the satisfactions of intimacy. It is as though, the psychoanalysts are saying, we have got our kindness wrong, that the ways in which we have described what we have in common, what holds us together, what keeps us keen on each other, have actually precluded our being together. That the kindnesses we have inherited are unsuited to the modern world, have even in fact—in their most sentimentalized versions—become estrangement techniques. Love freed from hatred kills fellow feeling. If there is a kindness instinct, it is going to have to take onboard ambivalence in human relations. It is kind to be able to bear conflict, in oneself and others; it is kind, to oneself and others, to forgo magic and sentimentality for reality. It is kind to see individuals as they are, rather than how we might want them to be; it is kind to care for people just as we find them.

V

Modern Kindness

"A sign of health in the mind," Donald Winnicott wrote in 1970, "is the ability of one individual to enter imaginatively and accurately into the thoughts and feelings and hopes and fears of another person; also to allow the other person to do the same to us." To live well, we must be able to imaginatively identify with other people, and allow them to identify with us. Unkindness involves a failure of the imagination so acute that it threatens not just our happiness but our sanity. Caring about others, as Jean-Jacques Rousseau argued, is what makes us fully human. We depend on each other not just for our survival but for our very being. The self without sympathetic attachments is either a fiction or a lunatic.

Modern Western society resists this fundamental truth, valuing independence above all things. Needing others is perceived as a weakness. Only small children, the sick, and the very elderly are permitted dependence on others; for everyone else, self-sufficiency and autonomy are cardinal virtues. Dependence is scorned even in intimate relationships, as though dependence were incompatible with self-reliance rather than the only thing that makes it possible. The ideal lover or spouse is a freewheeling agent for whom the giving and taking of love is a disposable lifestyle option; neediness, even in this arena of intense desires and longings, is ultimately contemptible.

But we are all dependent creatures, right to the core. For most of Western history this has been widely acknowledged. Even the Stoics—those avatars of self-reliance—recognized man's innate need for other people as purveyors and objects of kindness. "Individualism" is a very recent phenomenon. The Enlightenment, generally perceived as the origin of Western individualism, promoted "social affections" against "private interests." Victorianism, individualism's so-called golden age, witnessed a fierce clash between champions and critics of commercial individualism. In the early 1880s the historian and Christian activist Arnold Toynbee, in a series of public lectures on the Industrial Revolution, tore into the egoistic vision of man preached by prophets of free-enterprise capitalism. The "world of gold-seeking animals, stripped of every human affection" envisaged by free marketeers was "less real than the island of Lilliput," Toynbee snorted. American Transcendentalists of the same period attacked the spirit of "selfish competition," and established communities of "brotherly cooperation." Even Charles Darwin, that darling of modern individualists, strongly rejected the view of mankind as primarily selfish, arguing for the existence of other-regarding instincts as powerful as self-regarding ones. Sympathy and cooperation were innate to man, Darwin argued in *The Descent of Man* (1871), and a key factor behind humanity's evolutionary success.

Darwin championed kindness on scientific rather than religious grounds. For most Victorians, however, Christian *caritas* remained the epitome of kindness. Serving God meant serving one's fellows, through the vast array of philanthropic agencies sponsored by the churches. Secular individuals and organizations absorbed this ethos, with professional bodies emphasizing the altruistic motives of their members while politicians paraded their public-spiritedness. In Britain, self-sacrifice and social duty became keynotes of the "imperial mission," attracting hordes of high-minded men and women prepared to shoulder the "White Man's Burden." Meanwhile, across the Atlantic, an army of philanthropists descended on the poor, determined to elevate their morals while alleviating their hardships. Power suffused with kindly purpose became a militant practical force, molding social relations domestically and globally.

Today, these varieties of kindness are looked at askance. Victorian kindness is condemned for its moral self-righteousness, its class biases, its racial-imperial mentality. Nietzsche's sneer at nineteenth-century philanthropists as persons of "bad conscience" is widely endorsed. Nor did these Good Samaritans lack critics at the time—from Oscar Wilde, with his well-

publicized loathing of the "sickly cant of Duty," to radicals
and socialists determined to replace charity with justice, elite
kindness with universal rights. The horrors of the First World
War exposed the hollowness of imperial-sacrificial rhetoric,
while the erosion of traditional social hierarchies following
the war undermined the service ideal. Women who had long
touted self-forgetfulness and dedication to others as a female
duty, began to contemplate the benefits of equality instead.
Perhaps women were not always bound to care for others
more than themselves? "Poor-peopling," as Florence Nightin-
gale dubbed women's philanthropic labors in slum neighbor-
hoods, began to fall from fashion, and many welcomed its
passing, looking instead to trade unions and government to
eradicate poverty rather than softening it. By the early twentieth century, "good works" had lost their moral glow.

Kindness aligned to power degenerates easily into moralistic bullying—as many recipients of present-day welfare
services know to their cost. William Beveridge, the architect
of the British welfare state, was acutely aware of this danger.
Entering public life in the twilight years of Victorian philanthropy, Beveridge repudiated what he described as the "doing
things for other people" spirit of organized charity, announc-
ing his intention to approach social problems scientifically
rather than sentimentally: "I utterly distrust the saving power
of culture and missions and isolated good feelings." All human action was ultimately selfish, he declared. However, this
was not a viewpoint that Beveridge—a painfully kind man,

passionately committed to the relief of suffering—could maintain for long. His extraordinary 1942 *Report*, laying out the principles of cradle-to-grave welfare provision, was hailed by admirers as "practical benevolence." He began political life as a liberal, and ended it as a socialist committed to the altruistic values he had earlier dismissed, eulogizing the "spirit of social conscience" as the foundation stone of a good society. "The happiness or unhappiness of the society in which we live depends upon ourselves as citizens."

The kindness that Beveridge favored was determinedly modern and demotic, *caritas* without the condescending coerciveness of Victorian philanthropy. For his friend and brother-in-law, the Christian socialist Richard Tawney, kindness of this order required equality. Inequalities—of wealth, privilege, opportunity—were inimical to fellow feeling. The "religion of inequality" worshipped in Britain, Tawney wrote in 1931, "vulgarised" and "depressed" all human relations. His sentiments strongly influenced the labor movement, undermining free-market ideology and bolstering support for welfare principles.

In the event, Beveridge's welfare system did not create equality. The new public services and benefits introduced in postwar Britain reinforced many existing inequities. Yet the vision of a kindly state dedicated to universal well-being was not merely utopian. The creation of the National Health Service in particular dramatically improved the lives of most Britons. The values associated with the NHS—service on the basis of common human needs, equal treatment irrespective of ability to pay—commanded widespread allegiance in 1948, and still do so today, despite a host of destructive "reforms" aimed at undermining them. The present-day NHS is in many respects an archaism, a dinosaur of public altruism that stubbornly refuses to lie down and die. Strenuous attempts by succeeding governments to commercialize it have done much damage, yet the caring ethos survives, testimony to what Richard Titmuss, one of the NHS's most influential champions, described as the universal human impulse to "help strangers." Why should anyone care whether a person entirely unknown to them gets the health care he or she needs? On the Hobbesian model of human nature this makes no sense at all; yet the evidence that people *do* care, Titmuss believed, is overwhelming.

In 1970 Titmuss published *The Gift Relationship*, his famous study of British blood donors that showed the ongoing importance of kindness to the National Health Service. Asked why they gave blood, 98.2 percent of donors said they did it to assist someone whom they would never meet. "Sick people can't get out of bed to ask you for a pint to save their life so I came forword [*sic*] in hope to help somebody," one woman wrote on the study questionnaire. People who behaved in this fashion, according to Titmuss, were simply enacting a "fundamental truth" of human existence, that "to love oneself, one must love strangers." The good society was one that built on this truth, creating welfare systems based on the recognition that all people are dependent creatures, needing each other for support and comfort. A bad society was one that, in the name of freedom and independence, denied people the "right to give."

Like his friend and fellow social democrat Richard Tawney, Titmuss was a fierce enemy of free-market thinking. Far from a realm of freedom, the private market is profoundly coercive, he argued, forcing people into situations that thwart their natural altruism. *The Gift Relationship* condemned the American practice of paying for blood, which, by eliminating the need for personal generosity, undermined human fellowship. The commercialization of what ought to be a gift relation estranged people from each other, Titmuss insisted. The "universal stranger" (that is, all of us in our dependent relations on each other) became no longer an object of solicitude but an alien being, and communal ties were fatally eroded.

The Gift Relationship was enormously influential, and remains a revered text in social welfare circles. But it is also a poignant work, Canute-like in its defiance of the rising tide of privatization that, in the decades since its publication, has swept through the public sector. Margaret Thatcher's 1979 electoral victory marked the defeat in Britain of the Beveridge/Tawney/Titmuss vision of a kindly society, while the rise of Reaganism in 1980s America saw a similar erosion of welfare values there. Kindness was downgraded into a minority motivation, suitable only for parents (especially mothers), "care professionals," and assorted sandal-wearing do-gooders. The "caring, sharing" 1990s proclaimed a return to community values, but this proved to be rhetorical flimflam as Thatcher and Reagan's children came of age, steeped in free-market ideology and with barely a folk memory of the midcentury welfare vision. With the 1997 triumph of New Labour in Britain, and George W. Bush's election to the American presidency in 2000, competitive individualism became the ruling consensus. The taboo surrounding dependency became even stronger, as politicians, employers, and a motley array of well-fed moralists harangued the poor and vulnerable on the virtues of self-reliance. Prime Minister Tony Blair called for "compassion with a hard edge" to replace the softening variety advocated by his predecessors. "The new welfare state must encourage work not dependency," he declared, as a plague of cost-cutting managers chomped away at Britain's social services.

Meanwhile, "care" was becoming the new buzzword. Today it is everywhere. In the British public sector, "care providers" deliver "care packages" according to fixed criteria applied by "care assessors." In 2007, Blair's government issued an instruction to NHS nurses to smile. A cabinet spokesman explained, "One of the things that came out of the focus group discussions was that they didn't feel nurses gave the impression that they cared enough. They felt, for example, that they should smile more." This was followed by the announcement that nurses' smileyness ("empathic care") would be measured and the scores published on an online "compassion index." "If some jumped-up bean-counter comes near me with a 'compassion index,'" a nurse blogged on the *Guardian* Web site, "he'll get it administered rectally."

Public "customer-service" diktats like these are cartoon versions of policies in the private sector, where caring behavior has long been de rigueur. Workers in the burgeoning call-center industry receive training in "warmth" and "empathy," while Wal-Mart employees (Asda UK) sport "Happy to Help" badges. Corporations hire "emotional intelligence" experts to test the "empathic capabilities" of managers. One big American EI company (TalentSmart) claims to test the employees of 75 percent of Fortune 500 companies. An eye-opening report on British work culture by the journalist Madeleine Bunting (*Willing Slaves*, 2004) describes the "empathy audits" carried out by management consultants Harding & Yorke for hundreds of major companies. Employees are taped and the recordings analyzed for their empathy quota. "Sincerity is a big thing for us," one of the Harding & Yorke consultants told Bunting.

The ironies are not subtle ones. Capitalism is no system for the kindhearted. Even its devotees acknowledge this while insisting that, however tawdry capitalist motives may be, the results are socially beneficial. Untrammeled free enterprise generates wealth and happiness for all. Like all utopian faiths, this is largely delusory. Free markets erode the societies that harbor them. The great paradox of modern capitalism, the ex-Thatcherite John Gray has pointed out (in *False Dawn*, 1998), is that it undermines the very social institutions on

which it once relied—family, career, community. In today's
Britain, one in two marriages end in divorce, and one in four
children is raised by a single parent (nearly always the
mother). The percentage of British households containing no
working person (14 percent) has doubled since 1974. American marriages collapse at an even higher rate than British
ones, while 38 percent of American families are headed by a
single parent (84 percent by a female parent)—three times
higher than in 1970. Twenty percent of American families
have no employed members. Among those who are employed, stable careers—jobs for life—have been replaced by
freelance work or short-term contracts, long hours, enforced
mobility, and chronic insecurity. Communities built around
stable home and work relationships have crumbled under
these changes.

For increasing numbers of Britons and Americans, the
"enterprise culture" means a life of overwork, anxiety, and
isolation. Competition reigns supreme, with even small children forced to compete against one another and falling ill as a
result. In 2007 the largest independent inquiry into British
primary education for forty years showed stress levels sky-
rocketing among children subjected to constant testing from
nursery school onward. The authors of the inquiry report expressed "strong concern" about these results. A 2008 leaflet
issued by the mental health charity Mind warned children
about the dangers of exam stress, from sleeplessness to panic
attacks, depression, and suicidal feelings. "Don't try to cope
on your own," children were instructed. Why do we permit

our children to be treated in this way? How has such idiocy become acceptable?

A competitive society, one that divides people into winners and losers, breeds unkindness. Human beings, we have said, are ambivalent creatures. Kindness comes naturally to us, but so too does cruelty and aggression. People placed under unremitting pressure become estranged from each other. Like the bullied child who bullies others in turn, individuals coerced by circumstances become coercers. Sympathies contract as openheartedness begins to feel too exposed. Paranoia blossoms as people seek scapegoats for their unhappiness. Such scapegoating is a self-betrayal because it involves sacrificing our kindness. But this is a price many pay as tribal loyalties, sometimes vicious in their expression, replace wider communal bonds. A culture of hardness and cynicism grows, fed by envious admiration of those who seem to thrive—the rich and famous: our modern priesthood—in this tooth-and-claw environment.

Some kindnesses are perceived to survive. As previously discussed, parenting in particular is seen by most people today as an island of kindness in a sea of cruelty. But this continuing celebration of parental kindness can be very confusing. People who need to be tough and self-promoting in the workplace are expected just to slough this off at home. This can be hard for men, but for women it poses special problems, especially for those women who, having rejected the old ideologies of feminine self-sacrifice in favor of the cut-and-thrust of the working world, find themselves looking after children full-time. The current flood of anguished press commentary from new mothers shows just how bewildering this transition can be, as women raised in the me-first culture abruptly discover the pleasures, and pains, of prioritizing others. And this female confusion extends further through our society, as women continue to find employment in the "caring professions" where, in defiance of budget-obsessed managers, they go on dispensing kindness for meager wages and little recognition. In the past, women's association with kindness was a source of some prestige, but now it is a sign of disempowerment. Kindness may be admirable but it's a mug's game.

What is to be done?

Nothing, many would say. Human beings are innately selfish and that is that; we must live with the consequences. Newspapers bombard us with scientific evidence to back up this pessimism. We read about greedy chimpanzees, selfish genes, ruthless mate-selection strategies, even about meerkats—those famously cooperative creatures—who instead of looking out for their fellows spend most of their time watching their own backs. Richard Dawkins of "selfish gene" fame lays it on the line: "Human society based simply on the gene's law of universal ruthless selfishness would be a very nasty society in which to live. But unfortunately however much we deplore something, this does not stop it being true." Yet Dawkins does not despair:

If you wish, as I do, to build a society in which individuals cooperate generously and unselfishly towards a common good, you can expect little help from biological nature. Let us try to teach generosity and altruism, because we are born selfish. . . . Let us understand what our own selfish genes are up to because we may then at least have the chance to upset their designs.

Although we must accept that nature makes people nasty, "we"—that is, altruistic people like Dawkins who somehow, mysteriously, have escaped their genetic destiny—can nonetheless set things right. Here we are truly in the realm of magical kindness, akin to the type experienced in infancy, but which now is required to overcome not just ordinary human unhappiness but the realities of human biology. The speciousness of Dawkins's diagnosis of the human predicament is matched by the absurdity of this solution.

Natural altruism, too, has its scientific defenders. Evolutionary theorists demonstrate the high replicability prospects of kind people's DNA, while neurologists report ramped-up activity in the posterior superior temporal cortices of the brains of altruistic individuals. A host of studies purport to show generous behavior among animals, especially among ants, whose willingness to sacrifice themselves to the needs of their colonies deeply impresses tabloid journalists. The underlying imperative in all these cases, however, scientists concede, is the securing of long-term interests, especially species reproduction. From a natural-scientific perspective, kindness is always ultimately "selfish."

Science may be the modern religion, but not everyone

trusts its pseudo-certainties or derives consolation from them. Many people still look to "Christian values" to resupply a sense of human fellowship, which, in a secular world, has lost its ethical moorings. But the Christian record on kindness does not inspire confidence (Jonathan Swift's "We have just enough religion to make us hate, but not enough to make us love one another" still seems apt); nor do most other religions fare any better. The contemporary spiritual scene, with its vituperative slanging matches in and between faiths, makes a depressing sight even for nonbelievers. Turkish Nobel laureate Orhan Pamuk writes in passionate defense of the "unique human talent" to "identify with the pain, pleasure, joy, boredom of others," including others whose attitudes one detests ("Identifying with someone is not agreeing with them"). But when Pamuk wrote from the viewpoint of radical Islamists (*Snow*, 2002), he was vilified as a "headscarf professor." Better, it seems, the cheap certainties of us-versus-them than any disturbing intimations of human fellowship across cultural divides. Hate and alienation today seem to be experienced as more comfortable, more efficient, than fellow feeling. Yet fellow feeling is what people want. Mutual sympathy and kindness remain great desiderata of social existence. How do we permit ourselves to have them?

As Rousseau, Wordsworth, and many since have argued, childhood holds the key. It is often said of small children now that they are naturally cruel, but it is less often said that they are naturally kind, instinctively concerned for the well-being of others, often disturbed by the suffering of others and keen to allay it. Nineteenth-century accounts of the "innocence" of children, distrusted today as overly sentimental, were also an attempt to speak up for children's spontaneous kindheartedness, which was felt to be one of the casualties of growing up. Loss of childhood innocence was, among other things, the loss of a more affectionately trusting nature. The child of the eighteenth and nineteenth centuries may have been greedy, violent, and fearful, but he was also someone who delighted in the well-being of his fellow creatures; someone for whom the kindness of others was essential to his pleasure in being alive, and whose own acts of kindness were not, in Wordsworth's words, "purchased by the loss of power." After Darwin and Freud we have more ways than ever before of describing our suspicions about our more benevolent feelings—and indeed, about children as innocent. But there is a crucial fact worth putting as simply as possible, one that we just can't get around. This is that the easy kindness of childhood, the virtual reflex of engaged concern that children show for others, all too easily gets lost in growing up; and that this loss, when it occurs on a wide enough scale, is a cultural disaster.

The kindness of the small child, we have said, emerges in the first instance as a reaction to his dependence. The child cares for his parents so that they can care for him; his "kindness" is a magical wishing-away of any anxiety or unhappiness that might interfere with parental solicitude. This magical kindness fails, and its failure is the child's first trauma, one that he never entirely recovers from. But it is from this failure that genuine kindness emerges, the sort that can accommodate hostility and conflict while delivering the pleasures of mutual enjoyment and exchange. "Bad" parents (parents who fear ambivalence, and who want magical rescuing from it) can prevent this authentic kindness from developing; but so, too, can a society that denigrates kindness as weakness, and rewards unkindness. Real kindness is not a magic trick, a conjuring away of every hateful or aggressive impulse in favor of a selfless dedication to others. It is an opening up to others that—in Rousseau's term—"enlarges" us, and so gratifies our profoundly social natures.

Many people today don't believe this story, not just because they don't believe the psychoanalytic account of child development, but because they equate all kindness with the magical variety. Human beings, they believe, are mostly either good or bad, and the kindness of good people—Nelson Mandela would be a favorite example—is almost godlike, an ideal far beyond the reach of us more selfish mortals. This makes the ordinary, unsentimental kindness advocated in this book difficult for people to believe in, especially at a time when competitive and tribal unkindnesses have become the norm. From Hobbes onward, skeptics of kindness have pointed to the evidence from human history to show that people are rivalrous, greedy, and violent. It would be a fool who denied this, but perhaps not so great a fool as the pessimist who pretends that selfishness is the whole story, who denies what every person, in some part of himself, knows: that feelings of connection and reciprocity are among the greatest pleasures that human beings can possess. David Hume's irritable reaction to the Hobbesian skeptic—that in denying the possibility of kindness he had "forgotten the movements of his heart"—is as true today as it was in 1741.

The most long-standing suspicion about kindness is that it is just narcissism in disguise. We are kind because it makes us feel good about ourselves: kindly people are self-approbation junkies. Encountering this argument in the 1730s, the philosopher Francis Hutcheson dispatched it briskly: "If this is self-love, be it so. . . . Nothing can be better than this self-love, nothing more generous." In *Emile*, Rousseau made the same point in greater psychological detail. Emile's kindness, Rousseau shows, is an extension of his *amour de soi* (natural self-love). Emile "enjoys his *pitié*" because it expresses his vitality; only the self-caring child who enjoys being alive will "seek to extend his being and enjoyments" to others. Rousseau's portrait of Emile shows very well why it is kindness that is the most envied human attribute. People think that they envy other people for their success, money, fame, when in fact it is kindness that is most envied, because it is the strongest indicator of people's well-being, their pleasure in existence.

So kindness is not just camouflaged egoism. To this old suspicion, modern post-Freudian society has added two more: that kindness is a disguised form of sexuality, and that kindness is a disguised form of aggression—both of which again reduce kindness to a covert selfishness. Insofar as kindness is a sexual act it is seen as a seduction ("I am being very nice to you so I can get to have sex and/or babies"), or as a defense against the sexual event ("I'll be so kind to you that you will forget about sex and we can do something else together"), or as a way of repairing the supposed damage done by sex ("I'll be nice to you to make up for all my harmful desires"). Insofar as kindness is an aggressive act it is seen as a placation ("I feel so aggressive toward you that I can only protect both of us by being very kind"), or a refuge ("My kindness will keep you at arm's length"). "One can always, for safety, be kind," as Maggie Verver says to her father in Henry James's *The Golden Bowl*.

In each of these accounts it is assumed that we are self-protecting, self-gratifying creatures for whom kindness is one of our many strategies to secure our isolated and isolating needs. It is a picture in which our interest in ourselves and others is radically impoverished. Yet still kindness is an experience that, so far at least, we have been unable to give up on. There is clearly something powerfully preoccupying about people being able to take a sympathetic interest in each other, about our capacity to imagine the suffering of others in ways that can make a beneficial difference. Everything in our contemporary ethos makes kindness sound sometimes useful (that is, effective), but potentially redundant: a vestige from another time, or just part of a religious vocabulary. Yet still we desire it, in some way knowing that kindness—the unromantic kindness promoted in this book, which encourages a feeling of aliveness as compatible with, indeed integral to, a feeling of vulnerability—creates the kind of intimacy, the kind of involvement with other people that we both fear and crave; that kindness, fundamentally, makes life worth living; and that everything that is against kindness is an assault on our hope.

Telling people to be kind is never of course going to work (although it is possible to be shown the pleasures of kindness and the suffering involved in depriving oneself of them). Kindness can be a pleasure efficiently avoided, and one's capacity or instinct for kindness can be actively and unconsciously sabotaged by that part of oneself that fears the intimacies it fosters. Kindness, one could say, complicates one's relations with others in peculiarly subtle and satisfying ways; and for a very simple reason. Acts of kindness demonstrate, in the clearest possible way, that we are vulnerable and dependent animals who have no better resource than each other. If kindness previously had to be legitimized by a God or by gods, or located in women and children, it is because it has had to be delegated; and it has had to be delegated—and sanctioned, and sacralized, and idealized, and sentimentalized— because it comes from the part of ourselves that we are most disturbed by; the part that knows how much assurance and (genuine) reassurance is required to sustain our sense of viability. Our resistance to kindness is our resistance to encountering what kindness meets in us, and what we meet in other people by being kind to them. And, of course, our resistance to seeing the limits of what kindness can do for us.

So the pleasures of kindness advocated in this book could never be the pleasures of moral superiority or domineering beneficence or the protection racket of good feelings. Nor are acts of kindness to be seen as acts of will or effort or moral resolution. Kindness comes from what Freud called—in a different context—"after-education," that is, a revived awareness of something that is already felt and known. And this after-education, of which this book perhaps is a part, entails the recognition of kindness as a continual temptation in everyday life that we resist. Not a temptation to sacrifice ourselves, but to include ourselves with others. Not a temptation to renounce or ignore the aggressive aspects of ourselves, but to see kindness as being in solidarity with human need, and with the very paradoxical sense of powerlessness and power that human need induces. Acts of kindness involve us in different kinds of conversations; our resistance to these conversations suggests that we may be more interested in them, may in fact want much more from them, than we let ourselves know.

Acknowledgments

Our thanks to Judith Clark, Norma Clarke, Simon Prosser, and Courtney Hodell for their encouragement and helpful comments on earlier versions of the book.